A Step-by-Step Guide to
CAKE DECORATING
from Australia

A Step-by-Step Guide to
CAKE DECORATING
from Australia

Lucy Poulton · Sylvia Coward

MEREHURST PRESS
— LONDON —

This edition published 1988
by Merehurst Press
5 Great James Street, London WC1N 3DA
by arrangement with Viking O'Neil

Penguin Books Australia Ltd
487 Maroondah Highway, PO Box 257
Ringwood, Victoria 3134, Australia

ISBN 1 85391 029 5

Produced by Viking O'Neil
56 Claremont Street, South Yarra, Victoria 3141, Australia
A division of Penguin Books Australia Ltd

Designed and set in Australia
Printed and bound in Hong Kong through Bookbuilders Ltd

Contents

List of plates

Acknowledgements

I wish to thank the following for their assistance, help and advice and for making cakes available to be photographed for this book:

Members and staff of the Royal Agricultural Society of Victoria
Members of the Whittlesea Agricultural Society
The Cake Decorating Association of Victoria

I am grateful to the staff, students and friends of the Council of Adult Education for their encouragement during the preparation of this book. May it be of help to my many students.

I also wish to thank the many decorators who so kindly allowed the photography of their beautiful work.

Introduction

Cake decorating is a fascinating hobby, enjoyed by people of all ages. It is not only a hobby but also a craft and a form of creative enjoyment for the decorator as well as the admirer.

I have included in this book many suggestions and ideas gained from my own experience and that of others, and have provided answers to some often-repeated questions from my students.

Cake decorating should first and foremost be pursued for the enjoyment of what we create.

As we progress from novice to become an experienced decorator, our aims and achievements are more spectacular.

Through this book we move from the early basics of decorating to the more intricate details seen in advanced work.

I am sure the detailed illustrations will help the novice to understand the directions given in the text. The colour plates of completed cakes will be of great assistance, giving ideas which will enable decorators to produce new creations.

It is my hope that this book will stimulate interest and bring many hours of enjoyment to all who try this craft.

Lucy Poulton

Equipment

In this chapter you will find a list of the equipment you will need for your cake decorating work. (Note that measurements throughout this book are given in metrics for simplicity. Tables for converting metric measures to imperial measures are given on page 134.)

The best equipment for cake decorating is usually the simplest. While there are many items available in the stores, some of which are very useful for speed, the best results are often achieved with improvised items.

The following items are only suggestions and most decorators will soon adapt this list to their own needs. Those who wish to keep equipment to a minimum will find the first fourteen items are the only absolute essentials.

For piping work

1 *Icing tubes* Of the large range of sizes that are available, I prefer to use numbers 000 — 00 — 1 for writing. *Petal tubes* number 20 extra small or medium. These are available for right-hand or left-hand users. *Star tubes* numbers 5 and 8.

2 *Icing nail* This can be purchased or made by soldering a nail to the underside of a metal bottle top. It is used for piping flowers.

3 *Roll of waxed lunch wrap* (305 mm x 35 metres). This is mainly used for making piped flowers and lace.

4 *Small fine metal skewer* Approximately 10 cm x 1.5 mm thick — a hat pin will do if you can't get a skewer.

6 *Eye dropper* for liquid colours.

7 *Several sheets of parchmentene paper* Approximately 460 mm x 700 mm or, if unavailable, one roll of good quality grease-proof paper (350 mm x 35 metres). Refer to cone making (page 3). If preferred use Jaconette bags.

8 *A variety of colours* This may be as few or as many as desired. Small bottles of *liquid food colour* are readily available at health food stores or at cake decorating supply stores. Other types of colours are:

Paste colours

Powder colours Dissolve these in a little boiling water before using.

Non-toxic pastels or chalks These are available at art supply stores. To use, gently scrape the stick of pastel with a sharp knife on a saucer or bowl. Use this powder either dry to highlight tones and shading in flowers or flood work or, if desired, use as a liquid by adding water or methylated spirits. I use a variety of all of these colours depending on what effect I wish to achieve. It is sometimes a good idea to test colour combinations in a glass of water to see what colours can be achieved by gradually increasing or decreasing the amount of each colour.

Black is sometimes difficult to buy. This is made by mixing a drop of all your colours together.

Brown is predominantly a blend of red and green. I often use a drop of caramel to soften the harsh raw look of some colours.

Green is best achieved by mixing varying amounts of green, brown and yellow to get a good variety of realistic greens.

It is preferable to use a range of soft pastel colours, as too harsh a colour scheme on either cake icing or moulded flowers will spoil all the effort that has gone into the making. Practise colour matching and blending on scraps first. Some darker tones are often needed to keep a colour scheme from being too pale, but it is better to add darker tones gradually, because once there they cannot be removed.

Do not colour work under artificial light as this gives a deceptive range of colour. It is essential to colour in natural daylight. (See colour and shading page 125.)

1

For moulded work

9 *A small pair of very fine sharp pointed scissors,* flat not curved. These are expensive but will enable you to mould flowers, so do not spoil them by using to cut wire or other thick items.

10 *Tweezers* To help place stamens and arrange flowers.

11 *Scalpel or art knife* If these items are unavailable use a scalpel blade which has been placed in a cork top to enable easy use.

12 *Paint brushes* Obtain the best natural sable brushes you can afford. These are best purchased from an art store. Numbers 000 — 1 and 3 or 4 are the best sizes; these are used in floodwork and painting of flowers. One fine and one large brush will be enough to start with.

13 *Modelling stick* There are many items which can be used for this purpose. A range of thicknesses and some pointed or rounded ends are needed. Wooden meat skewers filed down to various-shaped ends are the easiest to obtain. The ends of paint brushes are my preferred tools; some people prefer to use wooden pottery tools for a variety of shapes and effects. A modelling stick is used to shape, mould, stretch or enlarge gum paste (see Moulded flowers page 46) during the process of flower making.

14 *Hair curler pin* An inexpensive hair curler pin is very handy for making smaller flowers.

15 *Stamens* Fine-tipped white ones are the most useful; these are easily coloured as required using any of the colours and a little methylated spirits. Larger stamens can be used as buds for small flowers, to save making these. Save the centre, plain cotton sections of stamens to use when you only need short ones. You can make new ends either from royal icing or by dipping them first into egg white, then into some dry gelatine and moulding to a fine end.

On some flowers just the cotton and end is used, so that no tip is required. I often use these cottons as stems for very small moulded flowers.

16 *Cotton-covered wire* This wire is available in various thicknesses in green and off-white. Use as fine a wire as possible, depending on how small and fine your flowers are. If you cannot obtain the covered wire, try fuse wire. To get a realistic look, very fine strips of green tissue paper can be wrapped around the wire to give the impression of stems. White wire can be painted green if required by brushing with green food colour mixed with a little methylated spirits.

17 *Crimpers* Also known as *Clippers* these are used to press patterns or borders on cakes. They may be purchased in various sizes and patterns. Place a rubber band along the length of the crimper to limit the size of the opening to suit your needs. You can push this up and down as you wish. To ensure that the teeth of the crimpers remain free of moist icing keep rubbing them through cornflour while you are using them.

18 *Cornflour* This is needed to keep your hands from sticking to the gumpaste while moulding. I also prefer to use cornflour on my hands rather than icing sugar when kneading icing.

19 *Modelling board, tile or glass* (Tape the edges if you use glass) A dark shiny wall tile is a very convenient size (15 cm square) to use for practice in all piping work and as a board to roll out small amounts of gum paste (see moulded flowers page 46). Practice work can simply be washed off as required.

20 *Painting tray* This is used to mix colours; an ice block tray will do as well.

21 *New wooden spoon* This is used for mixing royal icing. It needs to be free of cooking oils and fats.

22 *Acetic acid* This is used to mix into royal icing to soften the consistency and also to aid in drying. Lemon juice may be used if preferred.

23 *Airtight containers* For keeping small quantities of icing, cornflour and gum paste handy while you are working. Note that a wet cloth or a layer of fine plastic must be placed against royal icing to ensure that there is no air in contact with the icing, otherwise it will form a skin.

24 *Sieve* A very fine sieve is needed to sift icing. If you cannot obtain one, use either a piece of silk to sift sugar or make up the icing and pass it through a piece of clean panty-hose fabric.

25 *Turntable* As you become more experienced in decorating you will find a turntable very helpful, especially when working on borders, extension work and lace.

26 *Rolling pin* You will need two: one very small and one long. The small one should be about 150 mm and the long one about 500 mm. An off-cut of plastic plumber's piping is very economical for both of these. The large is used to roll out icing for cakes and the small is for gum paste work.

27 *Ruler* To assist with sizes.

28 *Compass* For any circular or scallop patterns.

29 *Emery boards* These are used to smooth off any rough edges on flowers, bells or other icing or gum paste items. Very fine sandpaper can be used instead.

30 *Large scissors* These are handy for cutting wire, paper patterns etc.

31 *Oasis* (Florist's foam) Used to hold items while drying. An empty egg container is also handy to place items on, while they are drying.

32 *Cutters* Special cutters are available to assist with the making of moulded flowers. You may find it easiest to start with a cutter, then, as you gain confidence with the shape of a flower, to make them freehand.

33 *Graph paper* To assist with patterns for lace etc.

34 *Foil* A roll of good strength foil will be very useful to mould into required sizes and shapes for flower drying and support.

35 *Patty Tins* Or other similar shaped items for moulding flowers and ornaments.

36 *Foam sheeting* A thin layer is the safest item to use for transporting cakes. *Note:* cakes should be stored in the boot of the car or on the floor of the back seat. Never hold a cake on your lap in the front seat of the car, otherwise there may be no cake left by the end of the journey. These items are not all essential for cake decorating. Start with a few basics and enjoy making and decorating some cakes first before you decide which items are or are not needed. In time you will probably find that there are some other items not mentioned that will be useful.

Paper cones — icing bags

Cutting

Parchmentene paper

Step 1
Take one sheet of parchmentene paper (size 460 mm x 700 mm approx.) (see Equipment page 1).

Step 2
Fold in half to make the sheet 460 mm x 350 mm (see diagram).

Step 3
Fold in half again and cut along each fold line with a sharp knife. By this stage you will have four strips 170 mm x 460 mm.

Step 4
Fold in half in the opposite direction. This will leave you with eight pieces 170 mm x 230 mm.

Step 5
Fold these pieces across the diagonal and cut along the fold. (You will see that when the paper is folded in this way the opposite corners do not meet at the top points.)

This gives you sixteen triangles approx. 170 x 230 x 290 mm (see diagram). It is a good idea to prepare several sheets of paper at one time, setting some aside to be used later.

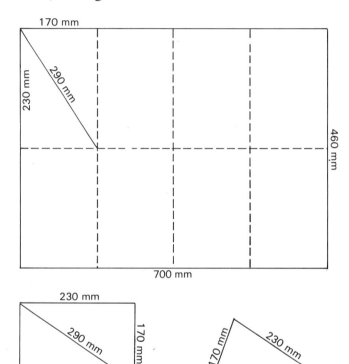

Parchmentene icing bags

Greaseproof paper

If parchmentene paper is not available, greaseproof paper may be used instead. As this is thinner, use a double thickness to give it sufficient strength.

Step 1
Cut a piece of greaseproof paper 350 mm in length.

Step 2
Fold in half and then cut along fold. You now have two pieces 305 mm x 175 mm (see diagram).

Step 3
Fold these from corner to corner, again noting that the top corners do not meet.

You now have two double triangles 170 x 305 x 350 mm approx. Use these doubled and fold to make bags in the same way as for parchmentene paper.

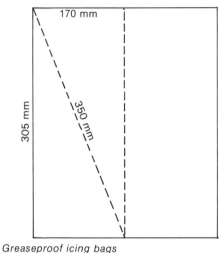

Greaseproof icing bags

Folding into bags

Step 1

Hold one triangle (a double one if using greaseproof paper) so that corner B faces the body and the short side is on the left.

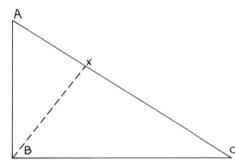

Folding the icing bag — Step 1

Step 2

Take the corner A in the left hand, fold it forward so as to form the first part of the cone at point X (see diagram). Corner A will now be in a straight line with B and point X.

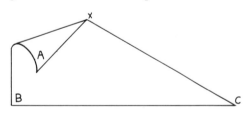

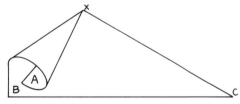

Step 2

Step 3

Now, taking corner C in the right hand, fold this over the partly formed cone. Turn the left hand over (see diagram) so that the two corners overlap each other at corner B. Note that there must be no hole at the point of the cone; also that the corner at B should overlap enough to allow firm support and some overlap right to the base of the point of the cone. The resulting cone should be wide enough to allow the width of 3 to 4 fingers inside the top of the cone.

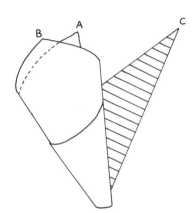

Step 3

Step 4

Take this cone in both hands and make one fold at the top, catching the three corners in the fold, then make another small fold over the first one. Your cone is now complete.

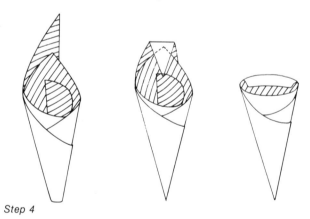

Step 4

If all the corners are not up high enough at corner B pull the inside corner (A) up a little to enable your next move to be completed. You will notice if you do this that corner C is lowered a little at the same time.

The size and type of icing bag used will naturally depend upon your personal preference. Jaconette bags are very convenient to obtain; they are already made and screw-on icing tubes can be changed in mid-use without the need for a new bag each time. I only use a Jaconette bag when dealing with a large amount of icing, such as for a shell border on a cake.

Using a Jaconette bag, whether it is made of plastic- or rubber-lined cotton, often ruins the icing because it becomes sweaty with the heat of the hand. This also applies to cream. It is also difficult to hold the end without having icing squeeze out all over your arms and hands.

As well as being more economical, it is also easier to handle a small cone such as a paper one. It allows better control and will give you better results. If a tube is to be used with a paper cone it is a simple matter to cut a piece approximately 1.5 cm from the tip of the bag and drop a tube into it so that two-thirds of the

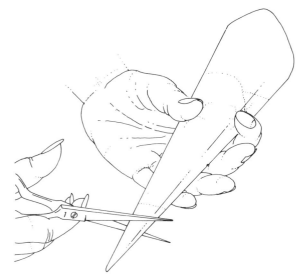

Cutting off the tip

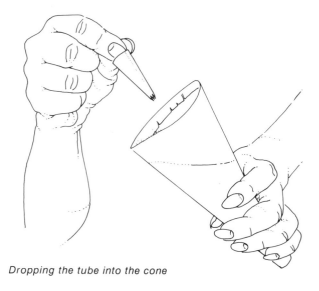

Dropping the tube into the cone

tube projects below the bag. When a new cone is required tear away the paper at the end where the tube is and start again. If you do not have a tube, a small hole cut at the point will do just as well for writing practice.

Butter icing

Basic piping techniques

(Royal icing may be used if preferred.)
N.B. When working with any icing, do not lick your fingers, knife, spoon or tubes. Keep a damp cloth next to you for wiping hands etc.

Butter Icing

See recipe page 128.

Colouring butter icing

• *Using paste colourings*
Using a knife or toothpick mix a very small amount of colouring into a small quantity of icing on the side of the bowl. When this is thoroughly blended mix it into a batch to be coloured. It is better to start with a little colour and to add more, rather than to start with too bright a colour.

• *Using liquid colourings*
Using a few drops at a time (an eye dropper is ideal), mix the colouring into a small quantity of icing on the side of the bowl and then add this to the full batch until the whole lot is evenly coloured.

• *Using cocoa*
Cocoa can either be sifted with dry icing sugar or it may be mixed with a little boiling water and then added to the icing. If the icing is too soft, add a little milk. Butter icing coloured with cocoa is called chocolate butter icing.

• *Using powdered colouring*
Mix powder with a little warm water. Allow to stand for a short while to dissolve and then add to icing.

How to hold your paper cone

(See page 3 for instructions on making paper cones.) Letting the cone rest in the circle made by thumb and forefinger, put a small amount of icing into the cone with a knife. Try to avoid getting any icing on the edges of the cone.

Step 1
Press the sides of the cone together. If you have used too much icing it will soon be obvious. It is better to re-open the cone at this stage and remove any excess icing rather than have icing spilling out of the cone while it is being used.

Step 2
Fold the top flattened part of the cone so that the corners come over to the centre thus forming a triangular shape.

Step 3
Fold this down twice so that it provides a good flat surface on which to rest your thumb.

The filled paper cone

Step 4
Hold the cone with your thumb on the top and your forefinger and index finger on either side of the cone. You are now ready to start icing (see diagrams).

Facing: Butter icing cakes.

Photo: Richard Cutler

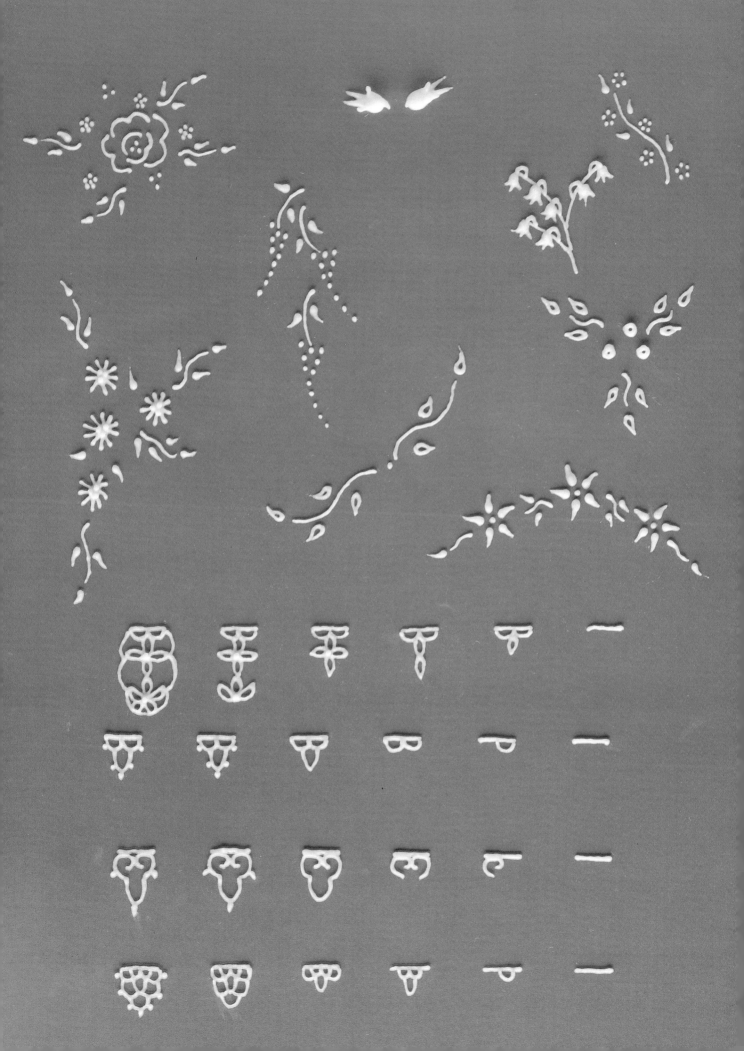

Note: When not using your filled cone, put the end of the tube into a damp cloth or sponge to prevent the icing from hardening and blocking the tube. Do not put the paper cone into the wet cloth.

I have found that the best way to hold the icing cone (or bag) is so that you can press with the thumb only and support the bag with the index and forefingers. Do not press with the fingers on the side of the bag as this will force the icing to squeeze back out from the top. Press with one hand only — although you may guide with the other (see diagram). While you are practising the exercises that follow, cover the rest of your icing with a damp cloth so that it does not dry out.

I prefer to use a smaller, broader icing bag than the one shown in the illustrations demonstrating piping techniques, and to hold it differently (see diagram below).

This shorter bag can be held comfortably in the hand. The thumb is placed on the closed top of the bag, thus preventing any icing from squeezing out over your arm as you work.

When working on piping exercises, I suggest you use the smaller bag and hold it as shown below.

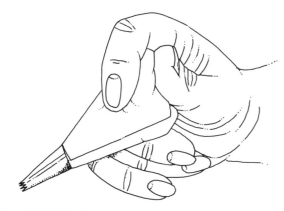

How to hold the bag

Exercises on a tile

Practice exercises are best worked on a dark tile which is easily cleaned. Practising on a tile enables you to make certain of mastering a step or technique before working on an actual cake. Butter icing used in these exercises can, of course, be re-used.

Facing: A few samples of combinations suitable for embroidery on cakes for many occasions. The lace patterns are only a few of the pretty laces seen on cakes in the book.

Trellis

Step 1
Using a small or medium (No. 5 or No. 8) star tube and a cone filled with butter icing, make four vertical lines each 40 mm long about 10 mm apart on your tile. Maintain the same pressure all the time — do not 'stretch' your icing.

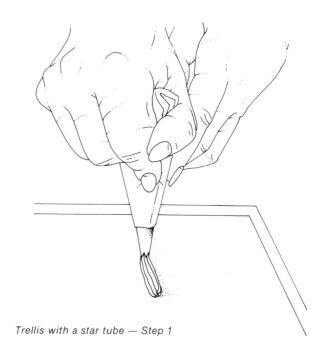

Trellis with a star tube — Step 1

Step 2
Next, make four horizontal lines across the vertical ones the same distance apart. Repeat a number of times until you can do it easily and evenly. Pressure on the icing cone must be kept even and the cone should be held at about a 45° angle to the working surface.

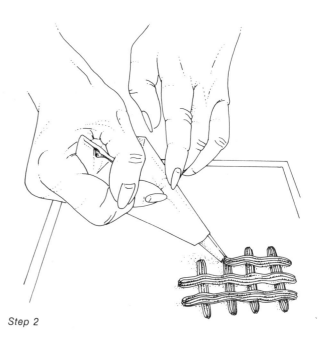

Step 2

Basket weave

Step 1

Pipe a vertical line about 75 mm long on to the tile.

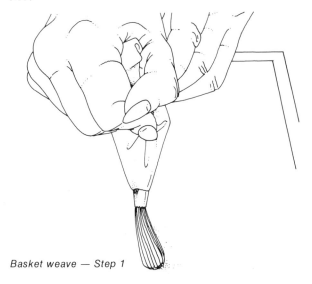

Basket weave — Step 1

Step 2

Make a number of short lines across the first vertical line, leaving a space the width of your tube between them.

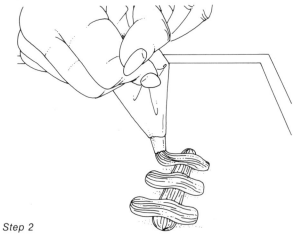

Step 2

Step 3

Make another vertical line just covering the ends of the short ones.

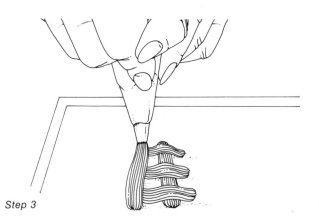

Step 3

Step 4

Pipe short lines over this vertical line so that the start of your short line looks as though it is coming from underneath the first long vertical line. Continue in this way, filling in all the spaces along the last vertical line.

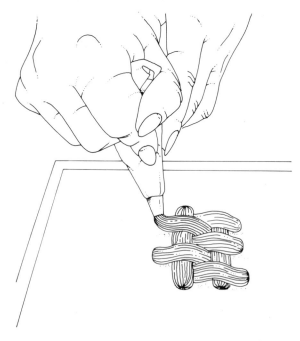

Step 4

Step 5

Repeat this until you have a piece of basket weave about 10 cm across. Start a new section on the tile and practise this until you are satisfied with the result.

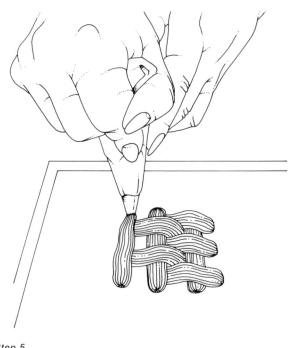

Step 5

Roping

Step 1
Fill a cone fitted with a small or medium star tube with butter icing. Hold your cone at a 45° angle and pipe a 'comma' curving the icing downwards, then to the left, then flicking slightly to the right as it finishes.

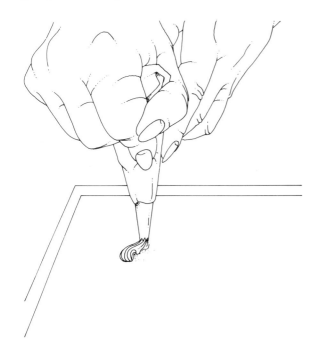

Roping — Step 1

Step 2
Make a row of these 'commas' joined together, remembering that every one must be exactly the same shape. Practise a number of short rows of this roping.

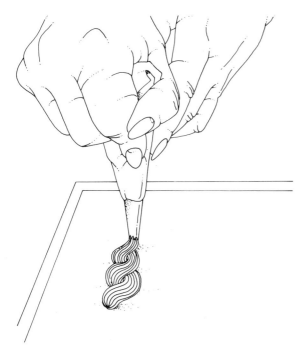

Step 2

Leaves with a plain cone

A plain cone is a sharp-pointed paper cone used without a tube but with the end cut to the desired shape or size.

Step 1
Fill a plain, sharp-pointed cone with green butter icing.

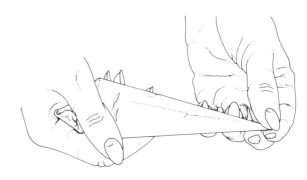

Leaves with a plain cone — Step 1

Step 2
Flatten the end of the cone.

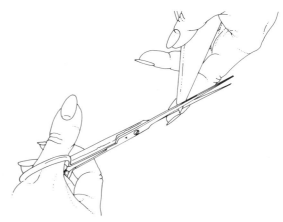

Step 2

Step 3
Cut the point to a V shape as shown.

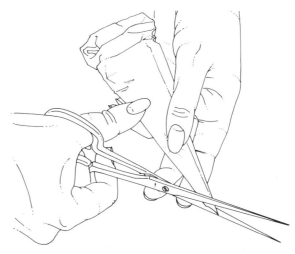

Step 3

Step 4
Hold the cone at a 45° angle and, with the tip touching the tile, press, allowing the pressure of the icing coming from the tube to move the cone backwards. Do not slide your cone along. The result is a slightly ruffled leaf with a central vein. Remember — press, ease off pressure, stop pressing and then pull away. Make several leaves like this until you have mastered them. To produce more ruffled leaves work with a forward and backward motion while pressing the icing from the tube.

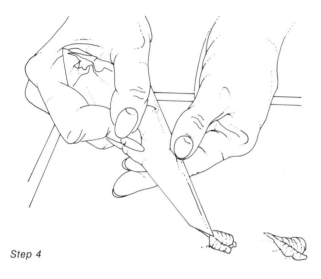

Step 4

Stars

Step 1
Using a small or medium star tube, hold the cone at right angles to your tile. Apply pressure, stop squeezing and then lift the cone from the icing. Remember — *press,* then *stop,* then *lift.*

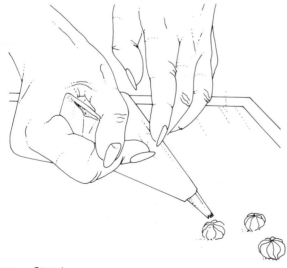

Stars — Step 1

Step 2
Make a number of stars in a row, evenly spaced and of equal size.

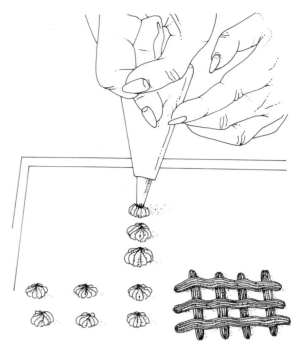

Step 2

Step 3
Now make a row of stars one below the other but gradually decreasing in size. You will see that the size of the stars is regulated by the amount of pressure on the cone. Don't lift the cone while you are still squeezing as this gives untidy points in the middle of your stars.

When you have completed these exercises, any left-over icing may be refrigerated in airtight containers.

Star tube roses

Put orange butter icing into a cone with a star tube. Keep the icing on one side of the bag only.

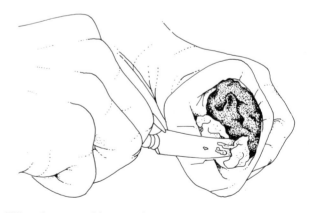

Filling the cone with two colours

Put some white butter icing into the other half of the cone. Holding the cone at right angles to the tile, press and move in an anti-clockwise direction about one and a half times. To finish off, stop pressing, but continue the circular motion of the cone for a second or two. Make a number of these roses on the tile until you are satisfied with the results.

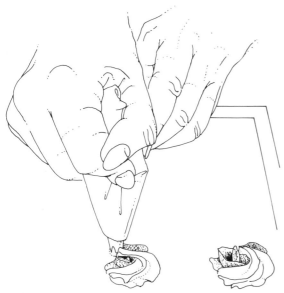

Star tube roses

Shell border

Again using the small or medium star tube, but this time holding the cone at a 45° angle, press very firmly with the tip of the tube touching the tile. Move the tube slightly away from the surface giving the icing room to build up. Ease off pressure, then stop pressing, tapering off the icing by pulling the bag towards you. You have now formed the first shell. Next, just touching on the end of the first one, start the next shell, ensuring that the untidy start of the icing does not show and again press very firmly and repeat the procedure.

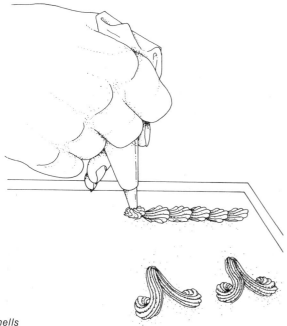

Shells

Scrolls

Step 1

Using your small or medium star tube, hold your cone almost at right angles to your tile and make an S-shaped scroll on the tile. Make a number of these scrolls until you can do them with ease and they are well shaped.

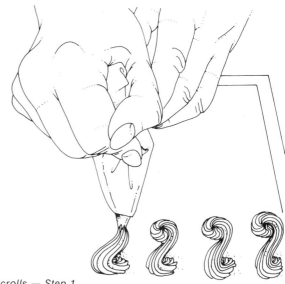

Scrolls — Step 1

Step 2

Make several half-scrolls as shown. Scrolls can also be formed with the two curls on the same side of the line — this is known as a 'C' scroll.

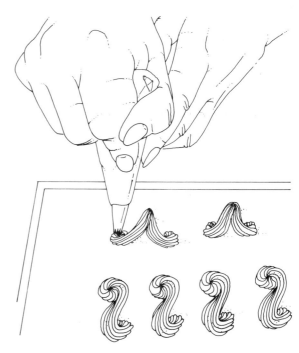

Step 2

Butter icing cakes

Three decorated butter icing cakes are illustrated facing page 6: Marble, or Feather Cake, Chocolate Icing Rose Cake and Scroll Cake. You may wish to try these first before going on to produce a variety of cakes for all occasions.

Marble or feather cake

Bake a chocolate sponge cake as one cake, or divide mixture into two 18 cm tins and bake in the usual way. Then sandwich the two layers together, bottom sides up, with jam, icing or cream. Note that the directions will be given for round cakes but you may use any shape.

Always turn your cakes upside down. Because the bottom is level it provides a better working surface, thus a better finished product. If the cake has risen too high in the centre, slice off the top to level it off.

The following tip will help you prevent your cakes rising too much in the centre. Cut a strip of towelling long enough to go right around the outside of your layer tin, its width twice the depth of the tin. Wet the towelling with water, fold it in half lengthwise and wrap it around the cake tin, securing it with a safety pin. Fill your greased and paper-lined tin with cake batter and bake. Add an extra ten minutes cooking time for a plain butter cake; about half an hour for a fruit cake.

Decorating the cake

Make up a batch of butter icing as directed on page 128 using 525 g of icing sugar. Make 300 g of this into chocolate butter icing (this is made by including 50 g of cocoa in the above mentioned recipe).

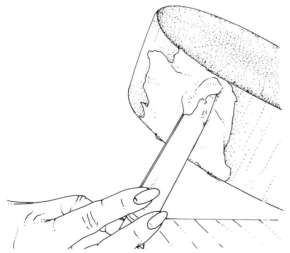

Coating the sides of the cake — Step 1

Step 1
Place the chocolate nonpareils in a strip about 75 mm wide on to a piece of greaseproof or waxed paper. Then soften 180 g chocolate butter icing with a little milk and spread the icing thinly and evenly around the sides of the layer cake.

Step 2
Holding the cake gently in both hands, roll it in the chocolate nonpareils making sure that the sides of the cake are completely coated.

Step 2

Step 3
Thin 120 g of your chocolate butter icing with boiling water until it is the consistency of a thin syrup. Pour this icing into a plain cone with a sharp point, then set aside.

Step 4
Crumb coating: soften about 100 g of white butter icing slightly with a little milk and spread some of this over the top of the cake to form a crumb coating, that is, a thin coating of icing that forms a base on which to work. This crumb coating prevents crumbs from lifting when you are working on the top of the cake. However, the crumb coating is not sufficient as a base in itself, and must be glazed.

Step 5
Thin 125 g white icing with boiling water, making it thinner than the usual glaze. Quickly spread this over the crumb coating on the cake.

Step 6
Immediately take your cone of soft chocolate icing and, starting in the centre of the cake, pipe a spiral toward its outer edge. Be extremely careful — this icing is very soft and easily runs out of the tube.

Step 7
Take a knife and draw it through the icing, starting at the outer edge and moving into the centre — you should not take the knife across the full diameter of the cake in one direction as all lines must be from the outside inwards. Then divide the cake into quarters and then into eighths. All this must be done while the icing is still wet. Put the cake aside to set.

Feathering the icing

This is one of the many designs which can be made in this way. Other suggestions are to reverse the colour pattern, or to reverse the direction from which the knife is drawn through the icing. You may prefer a herringbone effect created by piping parallel lines across the top of the cake, about 3 cm apart, and then drawing the knife across the lines at right angles, alternating their direction.

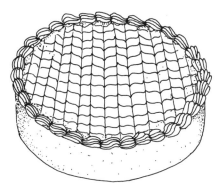

Herringbone pattern

Step 8
When the icing has set, fill a cone fitted with a small or medium star tube with chocolate icing and pipe shells around the top edge of the cake to give it an attractive finish.

Chocolate icing rose cake

Place a round single layer chocolate cake on a plate, bottom side up. Make a batch of chocolate butter icing using 500 g of icing sugar (see recipe page 128).

Step 1
Cover the cake with a chocolate crumb coating all over top and sides. (See previous cake description, Step 4.)

Step 2
Using a large, smooth edge knife and with a glass of hot water nearby, apply icing to the cake smoothing it all over with the knife. Dip the knife continually in the water so as to achieve a good smooth surface. Note that any residue of icing on the knife should be wiped clean each time. Apply the icing to the sides as well as the top of the cake. Set this aside until completely dry.

Step 3
When the icing has set, pipe 8 pink star tube roses spaced evenly round the top of the cake. Then on either side of each pink rose make a green leaf.

Step 4
Pipe a shell border around the bottom edge of the cake.

Scroll cake

Step 1
Use a 20 cm round cake. Make up a batch of butter icing using 500 g of icing sugar (see recipe page 128). Add enough cocoa to achieve a soft beige colour. Use half of this beige icing, softened with a little milk, to make a crumb coating. Add a little boiling water to the other half to make a glaze for the top and sides of the cake. Apply the rest of the beige butter icing as described in the previous chocolate icing rose cake. Allow the icing to set.

Step 2
Divide the top of the cake into eight then with a star tube make a scroll in each division, either a 'C' scroll or an 'S' scroll (see page 11).

Step 3
Pipe a circle of stars in the centre of the cake.

Step 4
Finish by piping a shell border edge at the bottom of the cake. You may wish to do this work either in white or chocolate butter icing. Any butter icing left over after decorating these cakes can be stored in an airtight container in the refrigerator. *Note:* Royal icing may be used for the decorations on these last two cakes. It is not suitable for covering soft cakes, however, because it sets too hard.

Royal icing

Note: Royal icing must always be kept covered with a damp cloth or plastic cover.

Royal icing

See recipe page 128.

When separating the egg, take care not to let any yolk get into the white. The slightest bit of grease can make the royal icing 'flat' and then it cannot be used for anything.

To test for 'flat' icing, put a spoon or knife into the icing and see if it holds a peak. 'Flat' icing will not hold its shape and will merge into the rest of the icing. It is also very shiny and wet looking.

Royal icing should be stored in an air-tight container in the refrigerator. Remove icing from the refrigerator a few hours before you intend using it and, just before use, beat it. If the icing is too soft, add more icing sugar.

For best results, make up the royal icing as close to the time it is needed as possible, then allow about 50-60 minutes to let the mixture settle. For floodwork it is best to let royal icing stand for 12-24 hours so that any bubbles can subside.

Different consistencies of royal icing are required for different types of work. Experience and practice will teach you when your icing is of the correct consistency, but the following guide will assist you at the beginning.

To test consistency, dip a knife or spoon into the icing, lift it out and turn it over. A peak will have formed on the back of the spoon or knife and it is this peak which shows how firm or soft the icing is. The figures below illustrate the different consistencies and how they are tested:

• *Lacework:* when a knife or spoon is lifted from the bowl and turned over, the icing should form a small peak, then immediately flop over. A 'line' of icing dropped across the icing in the

bowl should not disappear into the icing but should remain on top.

Consistency for lacework

• *Shells:* icing should hold a small peak when the knife or spoon is lifted out of the bowl.

Consistency for shells

• *Royal icing flowers:* the icing must hold stiff peaks when the knife or spoon is lifted out. For making flowers, it is best to use fresh icing.

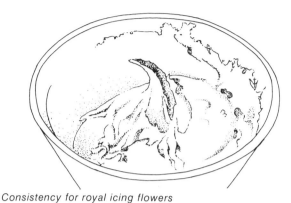

Consistency for royal icing flowers

• *Floodwork:* when a knife is drawn through the thinned icing, the resultant opening or line must have closed together by a slow count of ten.

Working with small and fine writing tubes can be most frustrating if your tubes keep blocking. A very good way of preventing this is to strain the wet icing through a new nylon stocking once the icing is of the correct consistency.

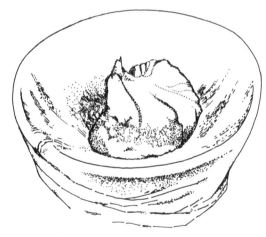

Straining the icing through nylon — Step 1

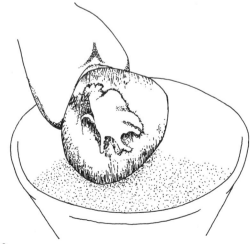

Step 2

Piped flowers in royal icing

Blossom flower

Fill a medium petal tube with pink and white icing, putting the pink on the side of the cone lining up with the wider opening in the tube and then adding the white icing.

Fill a small writing tube (or a plain cone cut to size) with green icing. Hold the cone between your first two fingers as you would a pencil, but using your thumb at the back of the cone to press the icing out of the cone.

Note: When you are making royal icing flowers, any size petal tube may be used but, of course, the size of the tube will determine the size of the flowers.

Step 1
Fix a small square of waxed paper to the top of the flower nail with a touch of icing.

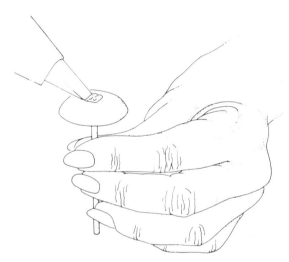

Putting the icing on the nail

Step 2
Hold the flower nail in your left hand (right for left-handers). In the other hand, hold the tube of pink and white icing at about a 30° angle to the surface of the nail.

Note: The scoop of the tube must be uppermost so that it is always visible and the longest point of the tube is closest to the body. The shortest end of the tube is therefore further from the body, and the seam (if the tube has one) is on the underside of the tube. The narrow opening in the tube must be slightly raised from the nail.

Press your cone, move the tube very slightly towards the outer edge of the nail and at the same time, turn the nail very slightly in an anti-clockwise direction (clockwise for left-handers). Now move your tube back towards the centre of the nail and stop turning and pressing. This is the first petal of the blossom.

Step 3
Repeat four more petals, starting each new petal slightly under the one preceding it. Take care with the last petal and lift your cone (not the tube) slightly higher, i.e. to about a 45° angle, so as not to damage the previous petals. A blossom has five petals.

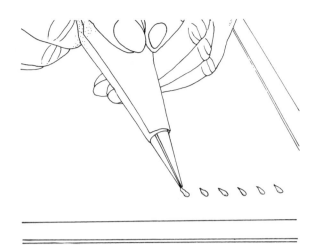

Teardrops for the blossom calyx — Step 1

Step 2
When you have mastered this, make three teardrops touching together at the base.

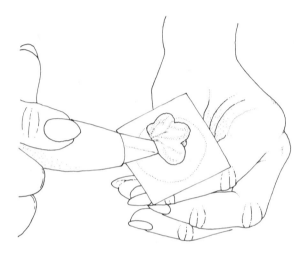

Making the blossom flower

Step 4
Using your green cone, make five *very small* dots close to each other in the centre to complete your first royal icing flower.

Step 5
Remove the waxed paper very carefully from your flower nail: hold a corner between the thumb and forefinger and then slide your middle finger beneath the paper to support the flower. Place it in a box or on a tile to dry.

Blossom bud and calyx

Make three petals as you did for the flower, and then with a small writing tube filled with green icing, pipe a calyx onto the bud as follows, or if you prefer, practise on a tile before applying it to the bud.

Step 1
Hold your tube at a 45° angle, just touching the tile. To form a teardrop, press your cone firmly and then ease off pressure, gradually tapering away to nothing. Refer to diagram — the principle is exactly the same as that of making a shell, except that this looks like a teardrop.

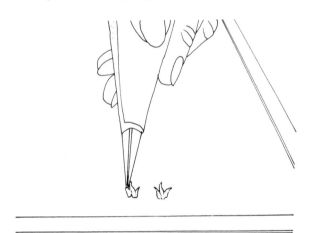

Step 2

Step 3
Starting at the base of this cluster, press *very* firmly, resulting in a large globe, stop pressing gradually and taper away, moving your tube away from the calyx to form the 'hip' of the flower as well as a short stem.

Step 3

Now that you have practised the calyx you can apply it to your bud by turning your flower nail so that the three petals are facing you upside down. Now, with the green icing, pipe a teardrop starting from the base of the first petal and finishing close to the top of the petal. Repeat on the other two petals. Turn your nail so that the petals are the right way up and then put your tube into the base of the calyx and press very firmly to form a bulb — then taper away into a stem.

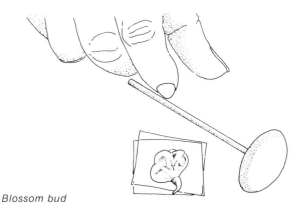

Blossom bud

To make a smaller bud, do exactly the same as above, but with only two petals. When making an arrangement of flowers on a cake, these 'buds' help to soften the arrangement.

Daffodil

Colour your royal icing yellow and fill a cone into which you have placed a petal tube. Fix a waxed paper square on to your flower nail with a dab of icing.

Step 1

Make six flower petals in the same way as the five you made for the blossom.

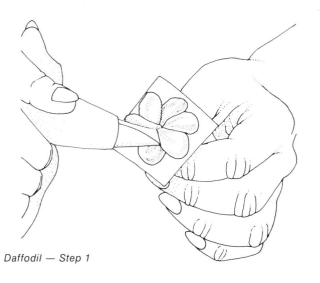

Daffodil — Step 1

Step 2

Holding your tube with the wide part of the tube touching the flower, on the side of the centre furthest away from you, press your cone and turn the flower nail in an anti-clockwise direction at the same time. Stop pressing when you have made a full circle and formed a 'cup' in the centre of the flower.

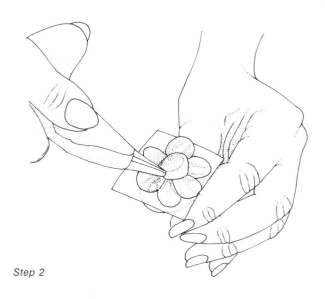

Step 2

Step 3

Slide the flower off the icing nail.

Step 4

Dip your thumb and middle finger into some dry icing sugar and then gently pinch the end of each petal.

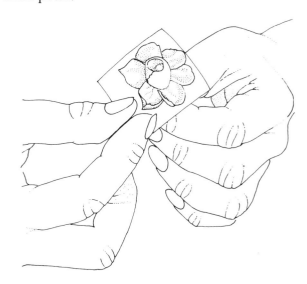

Step 4

Alternatively, the centre of the daffodil may be built up by piping a circle in the centre of the flower, using a small or medium writing tube. The circle is then built up in a continuous line, finishing with a slightly wider top to the 'cup' (which may be neatened off with a row of dots).

Daisy

Fill a medium petal tube with yellow icing and attach a waxed paper square to your flower nail. Hold your tube at right angles to the nail with the longest end of the tube towards the centre of the nail (the tube must be just above the surface of the nail).

Step 1
Start about 10 mm from the centre of the nail, press firmly, and move the tube to the centre of the nail.

Step 2
Continue in this way, working in a circle. Any number of petals may be used for this flower, but they must be of even thickness and close together.

Daisy

Step 3
When the petals are complete, make an orange dot in the centre of the flower.

When making the petals, take care not to 'stretch' your icing — you must press constantly. 'Stretched' icing results in thin petals which break very easily when removed from the waxed paper. Never turn your flower nail while making a petal of this flower.

Remove the flower on its waxed paper square from the nail and set it aside to dry.

Rose flower and bud

Colour 250 g of royal icing pale pink and stiffen until the icing holds long peaks when the spoon or knife is lifted out of it. Place in an icing bag fitted with a petal tube.

The centre of the rose: hold your tube against the waxed paper on the flower nail and at right angles to it.

Step 1
Press the cone, long end of the tube to the centre of the nail and, when the icing comes through, pull the cone towards you (think of pulling down a lever). When the side of the tube is touching the nail, turn the nail in your left hand in a clockwise direction, allowing the icing to wrap around the icing already on the nail to form a cone.

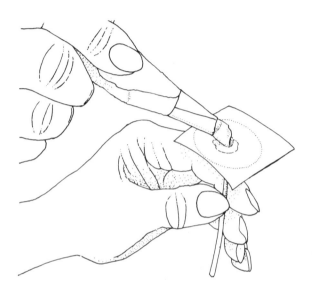

Rose flower — Step 1

Step 2
Finish off by turning the nail but holding the tube steady in the one position until you have completely circled the cone. Stop pressing, turn the nail and pull the tube away in the same direction, ending low down on the cone, close to the nail.

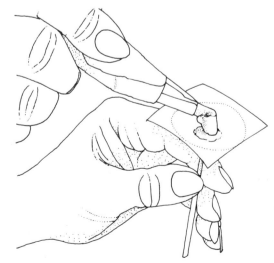

Step 2

Step 3

Continue building this cone of icing by wrapping another 'band' of icing around the icing on the nail. This is done by holding the icing bag at a 45° angle with the tube close to the top of the icing on the nail and almost touching it. This cone will form the centre of the rose. Repeat this process once more — the cone of icing should be 15 mm high.

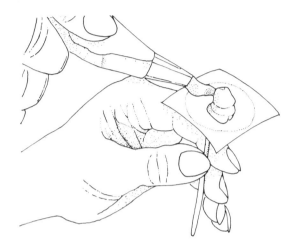

Step 3

Step 4

First row of three petals: touch the long end of the tube to the icing cone about half way up with the shorter part of the tube towards your left and away from the icing. Press and turn your hand from the wrist to the right in an 'up and over' movement, rather like opening a fan. Make two more petals in this way.

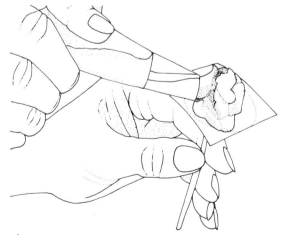

Step 4

Step 5

Second row of five petals: hold your tube in the same position as for the first three petals, but start at the base of the cone, in line with the centre of the first petal, right against the nail. Move up and over turning your hand from the

wrist from left to right and finish the petal. You need room for five petals in this second row, so make the petals slightly narrower than the first row.

You have now completed the rose. Carefully remove your waxed paper square from the nail and set the rose aside to dry.

The only way of perfecting the rose (or any flower) is to practise as frequently as possible.

Alternative method: another method used for making roses is to pipe them directly onto a skewer. These roses are usually smaller, so you may like to make some of each type to give some variety.

Step 1

Take your small metal skewer or hat pin. Place a piece of waxed paper on it. Hold the tube at the tip of the skewer so that it is at a right angle to it. Pressing your cone, and at the same time slowly turning the skewer clockwise, form a circle of icing around it so that the tip is encased in this cocoon of icing.

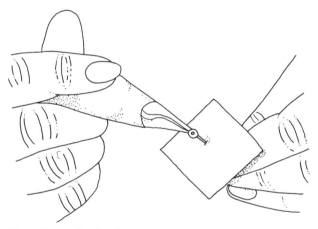

Alternative method — Step 1

Step 2

First row of three petals: holding the cone in the same way, press and turn your hand in the same motion as for the petals in the first method. Make three petals in this way.

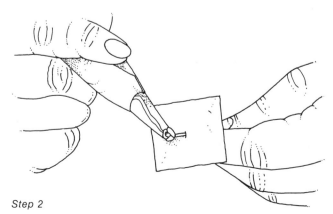

Step 2

Step 3
Second row of five petals: holding the cone in the same way as before, but this time allowing the petals to rise up a little higher than the first row, pipe five petals. You have now completed the rose. If you wish to make buds only by this method, stop after the first row of three petals.

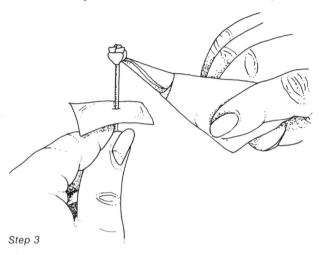

Step 3

Step 4
To remove the rose, hold the skewer in the right hand and gently slide the piece of paper up along the skewer length to pull it off. The roses will now be left on the paper. Be careful to hold the square of paper firmly as it leaves the skewer or the flower will fall. I find it best to pull the paper up using the index and forefinger together, and the thumb and ring finger together, allowing the paper to be between each pair of fingers.

Rose bud

Step 1
Proceed as for the rose flower, but after the first three petals shake the nail gently so that your cone falls on to its side and the V formed by two of the petals is facing you.

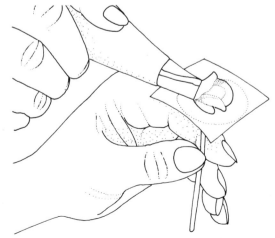

Rose bud — Step 1

Step 2
Using a hat-pin or skewer cut away the excess icing on either side of the base of the bud.

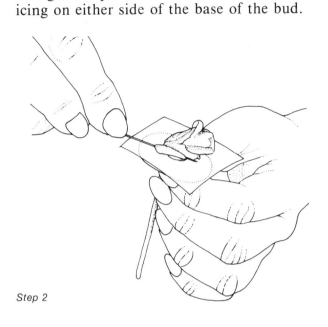

Step 2

Sweet pea

Fill a petal tube with royal icing. Touch icing onto your flower nail and fix a waxed paper square to it.
Colouring: Sweet peas come in many colours so you may wish to use a variety of colours. For a different effect you can create highlights of darker tones or of different colours in the following way:

Fill your cone with icing (white or a colour). Before you close it take your *clean* skewer, dip it into a bottle of food colour and push it through the icing in the cone so that you have created a streak of colour in one long band. This band should be along the side of the short end of the cone. Fold the bag in the usual way. Wash the skewer each time before you dip it into your food colour as, if particles of icing fall into the food colour, they will cause a fungus growth, thus ruining your colours.

Step 1
Holding your cone parallel to the flower nail with the long part of the tube to the centre of the nail, press and let the icing move out of the tube and onto the nail, ruffling slightly. Keeping the tube at exactly the same angle, move around in a horseshoe shape, turning the nail gently in an anti-clockwise direction when you reach the curve in the 'horseshoe'. If you are making a large flower, move the right hand up and down at the same time so that the ruffled horseshoe is deeper.

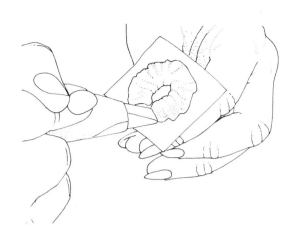

Sweet pea — Step 1

Step 2

Start again at the same point and follow your first shape. This time, hold the tube so that the short part of the tube is raised more than when doing the first part of the flower, making the petal curve upwards slightly.

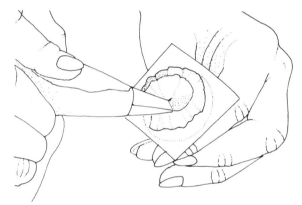

Step 2

Step 3

Holding your cone at right angles to the flower nail and touching the centre part of the flower, press the cone, moving slightly away from you and then back towards you, to form the central 'bud' of the flower.

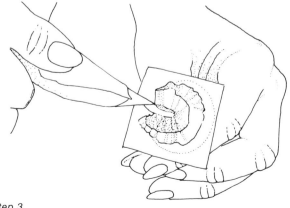

Step 3

Gently remove the wax-paper from the flower nail and set the latter aside to dry.

Violet

Step 1
Colour your icing violet and place it in a cone with a petal tube. Put a little yellow icing into a small cone fitted with a writing tube.

Step 2
On the flower nail, pipe three evenly spaced petals as for the blossom. Turn the nail and immediately opposite the three petals, pipe two longer petals.

Step 3
Pipe a small yellow dot in the centre. Remove the violet from the flower nail and set it aside to dry.

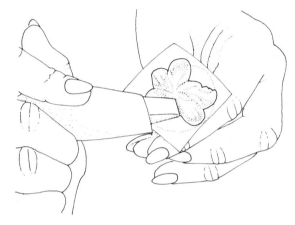

Violet

Wiring royal icing flowers and leaves

This method is particularly suitable for daisies, blossoms, violets and daffodils. Roses are best piped directly onto the wire (see page 22).

Flowers

Step 1
Using green florist's tape, cover several pieces of cotton-covered wire. These will form the stems. Hold the tape and wire in the left hand and twist the end of the tape around the top of the wire with right thumb and forefinger. Once the tape is secure, twist the wire into the tape, stretching the tape as you go. Make sure that the tape is as smooth as possible and that there are no gaps.

Step 2
Cut slits about 15 mm long and 25 mm apart along the length of a strip of cardboard and at each end make a fold of about 25 mm. Stand the cardboard on the tile on which you are working.

Step 3
Fill a plain cone with green royal icing and cut about 2 mm from the tip. Pipe a bulb of icing onto the back of each flower, then position a flower upside down under each slit in the cardboard. If you wish, you can pipe a calyx on the back of each flower (see page 16).

Step 4
Take a strip of wire, bend over the end to form a hook and push this gently through the cardboard slit into the green bulb of icing on each flower. The cardboard will then prevent the wire from falling over until the icing has set. Store carefully in a box until thoroughly dry.

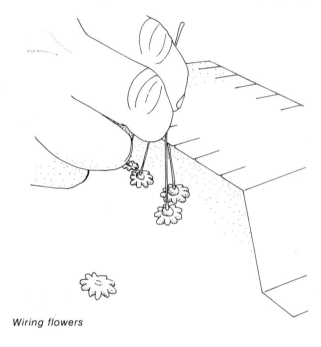

Wiring flowers

Leaves

Royal icing leaves may be piped directly onto covered wire.

Step 1
Lay your strips of wire onto a sheet of wax-paper and simply pipe the leaves onto the wire.

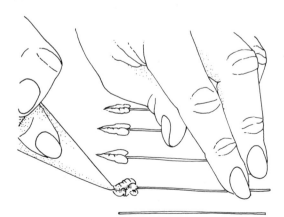

Wiring leaves — Step 1

Step 2
When the leaf is dry, turn it over and fill in the gap at the back of the leaf with icing and smooth with a damp paintbrush.

Miniature flowers (small daisies, for example) can be attached to a length of wire with royal icing to form a spray.

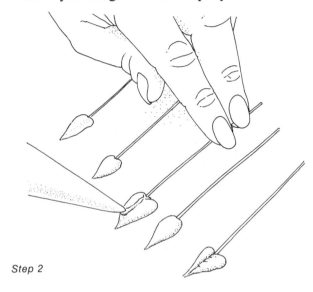

Step 2

Roses

It is better to pipe wired roses straight onto the wire.

Step 1
Bend the end of an 80 mm length of taped florist's wire to form a small closed hook.

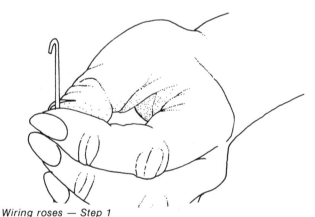

Wiring roses — Step 1

Step 2
Thread icing through the hook and turn the wire while wrapping the icing around it to form the centre of the rose. The rest of the rose is done in exactly the same way as shown in the second method of piping roses (page 19).

Facing: These fairy cakes offer a large variety of uses for the piped flowers and embroidery. They also give a practical lesson in the many possible ways they can be arranged.

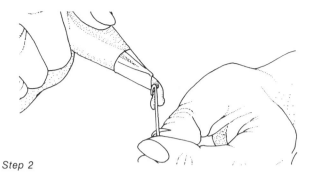

Step 2

Step 3

Push the end of the wire into a piece of Oasis or some other similar item such as polystyrene to allow the rose to dry.

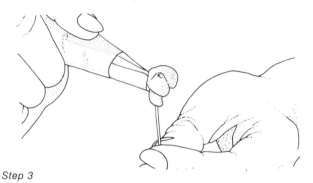

Step 3

Step 4

Using green icing, pipe a calyx as you did for the blossom bud, that is, pipe five long green 'teardrops' upwards around the base of the rose when it is completely dry.

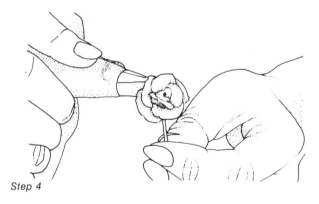

Step 4

Facing: The flooded train with bright carriages was made by Mrs June Hooper. Its bright colours and rolling curves would be a delight to any child for a birthday.

Mrs Valda Seidel-Davis has shown a beautiful soft touch in her picture of a little girl on a fence. The little boy in the foreground and the houses in the background all add to the delicate effect of this piece of work.

The little boy playing with his pull-along train was made by Mrs Robyn Nolan. This has strong colours and plenty of detail.

The circular flooded plaque made by Mrs Noelle Barnard is a good blend of strong colours and softer delicate shades. There is plenty in this picture to appeal to the young, and many skills to be acquired by the decorator.

Basic piping exercises in royal icing

Make up some royal icing as described on page 128. When you are using a No. 00 or 000 writing tube, try sieving your icing sugar through silk. You'll find this prevents the icing from clogging up the tube too often.

Fill a cone into which you have placed a No. 00 writing tube with white royal icing. The consistency should be the same as for lace work.

Exercises

Dots

Step 1

Holding your cone at right angles to, and not quite touching the tile, press your cone, stop pressing and then lift. The result will be a small icing dot. A perfect dot is nicely rounded with no long sharp point at the top. If you do have a long sharp point, either your icing is too soft, or you did not stop pressing before you lifted the cone. If the icing does not stick to the surface of the tile, it is too stiff.

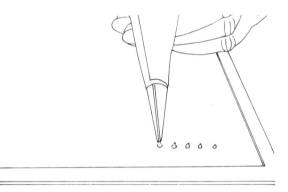

Dots — Step 1

Step 2

Make a row of six dots of even size and then repeat five rows below the first row, keeping the size of the dots and the spaces between them as even as possible.

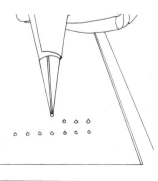

Step 2

Step 3
Now, exerting more pressure, make one large dot, underneath it a slightly smaller one and continue in this way until you end with a very small dot. This exercise is very important as it helps you to master the pressure control which is integral to any icing technique.

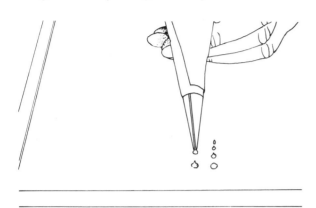

Step 3

Lines

Step 1
Using the same cone as that used for the dots, practise the following. Make a number of evenly placed vertical lines on your tile. Start by making a dot, but instead of releasing the pressure, continue pressing, at the same time lifting the tube from the tile and slanting the cone slightly, so that it is at a 30° angle. Continue pressing and bringing the cone slowly towards you.

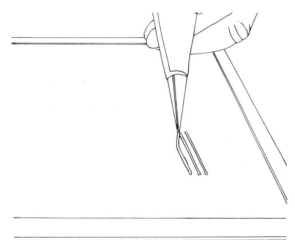

Trellis — Step 1

The result of this is a line suspended in the air above the tile, and attached at the point where you made the dot. When your line of icing is as long as you need, drop the tube down to the point where you wish the line to finish. Do not pull the line too fast or forget to press

continually on the cone, as this will stretch the line of icing.

Step 2
Make a trellis by piping another set of lines at right angles as seen in the illustration.

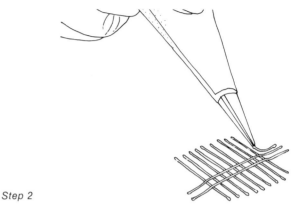

Step 2

Step 3
Using exactly the same principle, make a trellis at an angle but with the lines about 2 mm apart.

Loops

You may find it easier to use a piece of glass when practising loops so that you can place a pattern of loops underneath it.

Step 1
Follow the loops on the sheet. Here, even more than in the previous steps, it is important, having touched the glass to start with, to hold your tube about 40 or 45 mm above the glass while forming the loops.

Loops — Step 1

The most common fault in doing this work is trying to follow the lines too painstakingly close to the glass. This only makes your task more difficult. Keep reminding yourself to lift your tube higher, allowing the icing to fall into place in the required shape on the glass, and you will find you can do these loops successfully.

Step 2
Continue the loop steps on the sheet until you have completed them all. Repeat these steps until you feel confident that the effects required have been achieved.

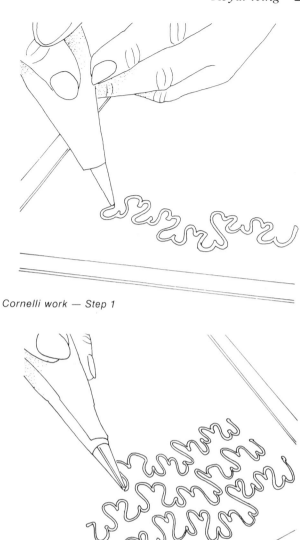

Cornelli work — Step 1

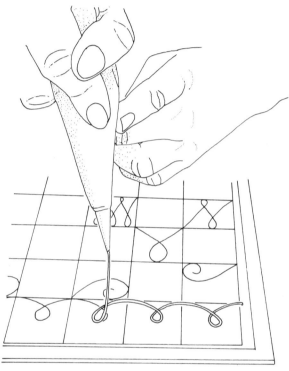

Step 2

Step 2

Scallops

Mark out a line of dots spaced about 2 cm apart. Take the cone and press out a dot at the first point. Instead of releasing the pressure, continue pressing, at the same time moving the cone to the right, allowing the icing to remain suspended until it reaches both the desired depth and width. Drop this scallop onto the tile at the second dot. Continue in this way until you have linked your row of dots with scallops.

Cornelli work

Using the same cone with the No. 00 tube in it, hold the cone at a 45° angle, pipe a series of 'm's and 'w's onto a tile in a quick, easy movement.

A characteristic of Cornelli work is that it *is* irregular, so do not attempt to make a regular pattern.

Beading ('the snail's trail')

This is used as a border or to finish off areas of Cornelli or similar work, or to finish off cake boards covered with icing.

Note: The consistency of your icing should be such that when the back of a spoon is touched into and lifted out of the icing, the resultant peak falls over at a 45° angle — here the icing should be slightly stiffer that that which you used for Cornelli work.

Using a No. 00 writing tube, fill a cone with royal icing. (Or use a plain cone with a sharp point cut to the size of a small writing tube.)

Work on a tile. Holding your cone at a 45° angle, with the tip of the tube or cone just touching the tile, press firmly and then ease off pressing, forming a bead or tiny shell shape. Continue in this way to form a row of beading.

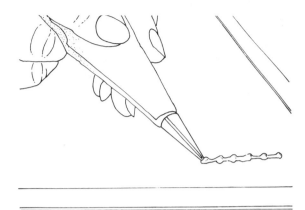

Beading

Writing on cakes

Lettering

This, perhaps more than any other area of decorating, demands diligence, concentration and a great deal of practice. Once you have mastered the basic technique, collect cards and magazine headings in order to increase your range of lettering styles.

Note: The consistency of your icing should be such that when the back of a spoon is touched into and lifted out of the icing, the resultant peak immediately falls over.

Fill a cone fitted with a No. 00 writing tube with royal icing. (When you have mastered the art of lettering, any size writing tube may be used.)

First practise freehand a row of continuous 'C's until you feel comfortable with the flow of this work.

Practising on a tile

Cake lettering

Measure the amount of space available and trace or print the message onto greaseproof paper. Place the paper on the cake and gently prick the letters onto the cake with a pin. It is best to use as few pinpricks as possible, although these marks will be covered by the icing. With your royal icing, follow the pinpricks forming the letters.

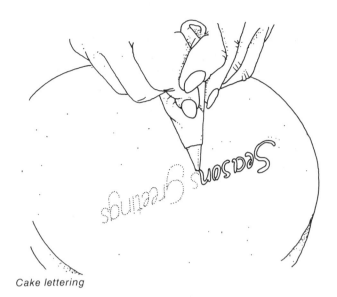

Cake lettering

Practise on your tile until you reach a point where you can work directly onto a cake without first marking the letters.

It is best to work in white icing while you are learning this skill. You can then paint the letters when the icing is dry. In this way if you make a mistake, it is easy to rub off the dry work and start again without leaving any tell-tale signs that you made a mistake.

Glass transfers

This is a valuable technique for transferring lettering onto a cake but it has many other uses.

Step 1
Decide on your lettering design. Trace it onto a piece of paper and then carefully trace the outlines on the back of the paper with a pencil. Place the back of the paper under a piece of glass so that the pencilled outlines are facing you.

Glass transfers — Step 1

Step 2
Fill a paper cone with a small writing tube with royal icing and then, *directly onto the glass,* pipe your back-to-front letters.

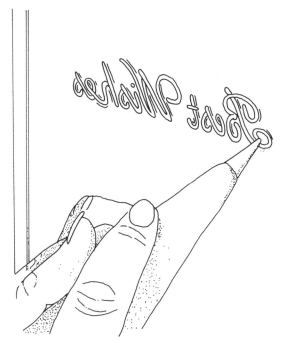

Step 2

Step 3
Allow the icing to dry and when quite hard, press the design against the fresh plastic icing. Lift the glass away and you will have your lettering on your cake exactly as you want it.

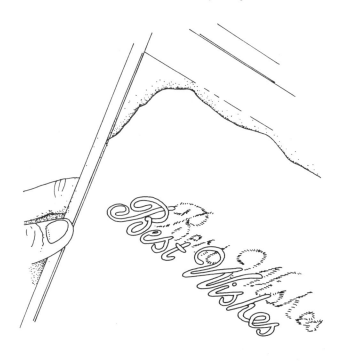

Step 3

Glass exercise

Place a tracing of the exercise sheet provided on pages 135-139 under your glass. See page 24 step 1. Working directly onto the glass, hold the cone filled with royal icing at a 45° angle and follow the lines of the letters. While the letters and words for these exercises are simple ones, more elaborate lettering styles may be used as you gain experience.

Lettering on glass — Step 1

Step 2

Embroidery, lace and extension work

Using your cone with the No. 00 writing tube in it you can now progress to an area of piping which can be most effective if used well. Remember that it is a good idea to use embroidery patterns to complement other work on a cake. You can also do this work on sponges and small cakes, as well as on formal occasion fruit cakes.

A few basic flowers will be described as well as the patterns of embroidery which are shown in the colour photographs. When you have gained confidence in this work you may wish to progress to a No. 000 tube. When doing embroidery on a two or three tier wedding cake, remember that the same *number* of designs should appear on each tier; the designs must be reduced in size to achieve this.

Embroidery flowers

Forget-me-nots

This flower is made up of five dots; you may or may not prefer to place them so that the dots are attached to each other. If you wish to keep the dots slightly apart, it may look better to add a dot in the centre of the flower. Remember to space the dots evenly.

Forget-me-nots

Snow drops or lily of the valley

This flower is another adaptation of the dot. Start by making the dot but enlarge it so that it is quite fat then pull the tube down and curve it to the right so that the result looks a little like a twisted tear drop. Stop pressing just as you swing to the right. Repeat, starting the dot on top of the first one, but this time swing to the left. Finally, pipe another dot on top of the other two, this time pulling straight down. Pipe a small curved line to represent a stem then pipe three of these flowers on the stem 5 mm apart. Finally pipe a small curved line from each flower back to the stem.

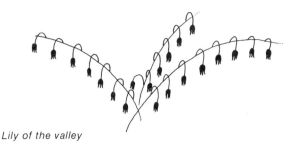

Lily of the valley

Hollyhocks

Using your No. 00 writing tube, pipe a circle about 3 mm wide, starting at the top and working in an anticlockwise direction. In this way you can ensure that the icing remains in a circular shape. Continue in this way until you have built up two or three circles of icing each on top of the other, thus forming a small cone or cylinder. You can either leave the hole in the centre empty, or else pipe a long dot with a protruding point into the centre of the cone. These flowers are usually presented in a cluster of three.

Hollyhocks

Alternatively you can adapt this work to represent broderie anglaise (or 'eyelet work'). To do this, the piping must be done straight onto a cake which has been covered in soft icing. Mark out where you would like the sprays of flowers to be. Then, taking your metal skewer, gently insert the point into the icing to form a small hole where each petal is required. (Don't make the holes too deep, or the cake will dry out.) Pipe one circle around each hole.

Broderie anglaise

Drag leaves or small piped leaves

These leaves are used extensively in many areas of embroidery; they can also be incorporated as flowers into some arrangements. Using your No. 00 writing tube, start piping as if making a medium dot. Instead of stopping, allow the dot to thicken a little; still pressing, taper away to a point and quickly (but smoothly) pull away so that a teardrop is formed. If you want your leaf to be very small and short, stop pressing sooner. Once you are confident about these leaves, you can use them effectively in groupings of five

Embroidery leaves

lines until they look like stems. It is easiest to pipe with the right hand and gently help the direction with the left hand. These stems may be combined with any of the embroidery flowers

Embroidery flowers

which have been described so far. Leaves, or for that matter flowers, can also be created by just outlining their shape. The drawing below

Outlined leaves

illustrates this. Pipe two or more gently curving lines to represent stems. Instead of using drag leaves, pipe a small, curved shape that looks like the outline of your required leaf shape. By combining a number of these together you may create another flower to add to your collection of ideas.

Outlined flowers

Blue-bird or dove

These little birds are very popular on engagement and wedding cakes. They can be piped directly onto a cake or, if you prefer, they can be made on waxed lunch wrap, allowed to dry and then gently peeled off and stored in a box or jar. They are often piped in white or pale blue icing; they can also be painted over with a non-toxic gold or silver craft paint (either all over or just on the tips of the wings and tail).

Take your cone fitted with a No. 00 tube (or if you wish to make a larger bird use a No. 1 tube). Using the same method that you have just used for the leaves, make a fatter, longer leaf shape. Instead of having only one elongated point, take your tube back into the centre of the dot and drag the icing down to form the second part of the tail. The two ends forming the tail may be spaced as close or as far apart as you require.

Holding the tube in the centre of the dot again, keep pressing, at the same time moving the tube up and down, to allow a fat dot (which is the 'body') to build up. Instead of finishing in the usual way, keep pressing and draw the tube away in a forward motion so that the peak thus formed looks like a beak attached to a bird's head.

To form the wings, pipe the next dot on the right hand side midway along the length of the bird. Again, keep pressing and easing your tube back and forth to allow the dot to build up a little; keep pressing while you pull away so that a peak forms on the end of this dot. This is the first wing. Repeat on the left side to form the second wing. If you would like to create birds with a more feathered look to their wings, you can pipe them onto waxed lunch wrap and then attach to the body with a little icing after they have dried. Pipe one small curved line, then a second in the opposite direction; now pipe another three lines directly underneath the one above, shortening each line each time. Do this for both wings. A tail may be attached in the same way if you require an upturned tail.

Bluebird or dove

If your bird does not look fat enough or is uneven, any of these movements can be repeated over each other, so you can even up an uneven tail or lengthen a wing or beak, as long as you do so immediately, while the icing is still soft.

Wings and tail

Easter daisy

This daisy consists of several short lines that meet in the centre. You can have any number of lines, depending how large or small you want your flower. Pipe a short line about 3 mm long, then pipe the next line about 1.5 mm from the first at the outside and meet in the centre. Continue in this way forming either a circular or oval shape as you progress. You may like to pipe a few small dots in the centre. Do this either in white icing or in a colour that blends with your overall colour scheme. To make a bud, pipe about five lines with a small drag leaf below them.

Easter daisy

Embroidery hints

You can get lots of ideas for embroidery patterns from embroidered tablecloths, sheets, table centres, baby clothes or even wrapping paper. The design of floral patterns used in a fabric or lace can also give you ideas. If I am asked to do a design for a wedding or christening cake, I can often get an inspiration from the design or pattern of the wedding dress or christening robe to be worn. The colour or design of the fabric of the bridesmaids' dresses can also help to create some unusual combinations. Do remember, however, not to spoil your creation by using colours that clash, or making your work too ornate and heavy.

Embroidery used in illustrated cakes

Often you will be impressed by some particular feature used on a cake, or you may be asked to decorate a cake in a style similar to a picture you have. The following describes some of the embroidery used in the cakes illustrated in colour. This should give you enough information to tackle some of this type of work.

Beige oval birthday cake
This has a very simple embroidery design which

Facing: This engagement cake, made by Mrs Maureen Ball, was exhibited at the Whittlesea Show. Floodwork has been used as an unusual feature. Note the pretty treatment of the posy of flowers.

Centre left, above: This cake, made by Mrs Dorothy Parsons, is a beautiful presentation of floodwork. Strong bold lines set in a background of delicate mountains and trees made this a very suitable choice for a man's cake.

Centre left, below: A pearl cake for a pearl anniversary was made by Mrs Dorothy Silva. There is plenty of skill evident in the decorating of this lovely cake as well as thoughtful planning. The pearly colours of the magnolias are complemented by the pearl drops seen at the base of each piece of lace, which in turn have been made in the shape of the flowers. The final touch is the cake itself in the shape of a pearl drop.

Centre right above: Soft colours with a design which complements the oval shape of the cake have been used here by Mrs Noelle Barnard. There is a traditional influence in this lovely cake, and it shows some unusual features such as the two-tone lace which has been placed to give the effect of extension work.

Centre right, below: Made by Mrs Pam Leman, this cake is delicate and suitable for any occasion. There is plenty of work on this cake but it is still soft and light. The moulded flowers used are very dainty.

complements the arrangement on the top of the cake. The embroidery is an umbrella in a soft shade of apricot. A brown handle and small pieces of lace forming a frill complete the design.

The daisies are made by outlining the shape of each petal, then using a dot for the centre. There are six apricot coloured petals and one brown dot in each flower. A butterfly is described in floodwork on page 41. See also page 33 for lacework and page 46 for more information on moulded flowers. The umbrella will be found in moulded decorations on page 104.

Pale green, scalloped birthday cake
This is an excellent example of how to use a theme on a cake. There are primulas in the moulded flowers on top of the cake (see page 46 for moulded work) and a pattern of dots and primulas has been repeated in the embroidery. This embroidery is all done in a darker shade of spring green. Note how very simple the embroidery design is. Each design consists of four primulas, with another flower at either side to separate each group. The flower is made up of the outline of a primula as seen directly from above: six almost heart-shaped petals, with a group of seven dots in the centre. The flowers are spaced by dots and there are small stems and leaves completing the work. See page 39 for floodwork.

Two-tier circular wedding cake
In lovely deep shades of pink, this cake has a complementary pattern of embroidered roses. These are outline roses, using a two-tone pink for the flowers and changing to a single tone for the rosebud. The embroidered leaves are in two tones of green. See page 33 for lace, and page 46 for description of moulded flowers.

Three-tier oval cake
This cake also uses roses as its central theme.

Facing above: The oval shape of this cake is a lovely complement to the cradle effect achieved by the baby playing and sleeping with his animal friends. Although there is plenty of blue in this cake, made by Mrs Robyn Nolan, it is still beautifully soft and delicate, combining many features of cake decorating.

Facing below: Pink, blue and cream is the colour theme for this delicate christening cake made by Mrs Wendy Fox. The fine work seen in this cake is beautifully soft in presentation. It also shows a good blend of lace extension work, moulded flowers and floodwork.

The embroidery on this cake combines small embossed roses, forget-me-nots, stems and leaves. The design is repeated on the pillars, which are handmade and complement the oval shape of the cake. The roses are piped as follows: three dots for the centre; these are then encased by a semi-circle or C shape. Double scallops are embroidered around this central piece to give a rose effect; four or three were used on these flowers.

Roses

Clover shape three-tier wedding cake
Four petal daisies and carnations are used in the embroidery on this unusual cake. The side views of carnations are used as decoration on the top of each tier; these are then complemented by smaller clusters of daisies on each of the corners below the sprays of moulded flowers. Very small, unusual butterflies are another feature. These are made by piping the body straight onto the cake and then attaching the wings later. Pipe a fat line for the body, making it fatter at the head, tapering to the tail end. Next pipe a pair of wings onto some waxed lunch paper. You may either do these freehand or draw them first then, placing the drawing under the lunchwrap, pipe over this. When they are completely dry, attach each wing with a small line of icing. The feelers are applied in the same way. The wings on this butterfly have a double heart shape. See page 46 for moulded flowers.

Butterfly

Two-tier octagonal cake
As well as an umbrella and miniature apricot roses, this cake has an interesting alternating pattern of lily of the valley, daisies and forget-me-nots. Sometimes when a cake has so many decorated sides the result can be heavy. This design, however, has a very soft touch and demonstrates a pleasant blend of moulded work

with embroidery. See page 104 for the umbrella and page 46 for moulded flowers.

Three-tier oval cake

This combines embroidered and moulded daisies to create a crisp, clean look. See daisy embroidery suggestions earlier in this section. For moulded bells see page 103.

'Comma' cake

This is an unusual cake in many ways. It will be of particular interest to the more experienced decorator who would like to become more innovative in style and presentation. Each tier is a comma shape, the centre tier reversed. The pillars have been made by winding silk cord around the skewers which support the cake. The embroidery is beautiful soft sprays of freesia; as you can see on the side view, the stems are cleverly integrated into the extension work (see page 34). All this embroidery was piped in white and then painted over very gently with a fine paint brush. The bridge of the extension work is in pale green with the remainder in white.

Four bells cake

This is a perfect example of fine, intricate work, a creation which any bride and groom would be proud to see on their wedding table. If you look closely, you will see that all the basic techniques can be found on this masterpiece. The embroidery is a rich blend of roses, forget-me-nots, daisies and small sprays of fern. The fern has been created by piping clusters of dots in long narrowing groups on small stems.

Fern

Embroidery flowers and fern on wire

Lily of the valley, forget-me-nots and hollyhocks

These may all be piped directly onto wire to give a soft, fine look to a spray of flowers. They are all made in the same way. Take a piece of find white cotton-covered wire. Dip it into a glass of water (this will allow the icing to stick more rapidly) then gently curve and lay it onto a sheet of waxed paper. Starting at the top, pipe three to five graded dots; now pipe the required flowers so that the flowers are lying partly on the wire and partly on the paper. Do not forget

to grade the sizes of the flowers also, so that the stem goes from small to large.

When each stem has dried (this will take at least an hour) peel the stem gently off the paper, turn the wire over and repeat the same steps on the back so that the flowers are piped back to back. Although these stems are very fragile they may be stored in a shirt box (or similar) lined with cotton wool, for safe-keeping until required.

Ferns

Ferns of various types may be made in the same way as follows: Taking a piece of green wire, dip it into a glass of water and curve. Pipe a series of green dots along the length of the wire. Grade these from small to large making sure that the icing is on the wire as well as on the paper. Take another piece of waxed paper and lay it flat over the stem, press gently to flatten the icing, but be careful not to press so hard that the wire shows through the centres of the icing. Set these aside to dry and do not peel off the paper until the fern is required. Experiment a little to create other types of fern, but you will find it hard to create ferns that are too large as they are inclined to break.

Ribbon insertion

Some of the cakes I have described have also featured what is known as ribbon insertion. This ribbon may be inserted and decorated with embroidery or, if you prefer, it may be left plain. (See the christening cake, facing page 31.)

If you wish to add embroidery work to ribbon inserts, the bell cake offers a good example of this. Ribbon may be inserted in wide or narrow strips after the cake has been iced and allowed to dry. Measure an area into which you wish to insert the ribbon, then mark out with a pin prick how far apart each piece of ribbon is to be. If the ribbon inserts are to be wide allow for this in your spacing. Cut a clean, straight line into the cake at each of these points (a scapel will make this job easier). Make the slit only a fraction wider than the ribbon you will be using and do not take the slits too far into the icing. If the inserts are to be narrow, take a small piece of ribbon about 1 cm in length; using tweezers, fold this piece in half and insert the two cut ends into the slit. Push the ribbon into the icing as far as it will go, so that it remains there securely. A little egg white may be used on the ends of the ribbon to help keep it in place.

If the ribbon looks a little flat, gently loosen it by passing your fine skewer through the centre of the loop left showing. If the slits for the ribbon are to be wider apart (such as in the bell cake) cut your ribbon wider (about 7 mm wider than the space required) and place one end only in each of the slits. This time it will definitely be necessary to moisten the ends with egg white to ensure that they remain in place.

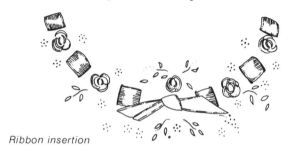

Ribbon insertion

Lace pieces

Lace is piped in pieces and then attached one piece at a time. The pieces must therefore be uniform in size and shape. A good way of achieving this is to use a sheet of graph paper to draw rows of various designs. This paper may be stored away for future use, so it is probably easier to practise and draw a variety of designs. To get new designs, look at some real lace; I will also explain how to do some of the lace designs used on the cakes illustrated. (See below for illustrations of lace.) For a base, use a piece of

caneite board (or a thick piece of cardboard will do). Take your graph paper with the designs drawn in rows. Place the graph paper onto your board then lay a piece of waxed lunchwrap, shiny side up, over this. Pin these down at the four corners. Do not insert pins into the graph paper, so that when you have completed the first row of lace, you can move the graph paper up or down to make as many rows of each design as you wish. Remember that you will have breakages with this work so it is wise to make spare pieces.

Using your small writing tube make lace pieces by following the designs on the graph. Holding your tube at an almost 45° angle, touch the lunchwrap with the end of the tube, lifting the tube as you press, and follow the design. Lace pieces are done in rows of ten to make counting easier when doing pieces for a cake. Move the design sheet along under the lunchwrap as you practise more pieces. You may find it easier to do the lace piece upside down, i.e. with the point of the design facing you.

Try to do as much of the lace in one movement as you can to avoid the untidy look of work with joins in it. Some lace pieces may look daintier with small dots on the outside line or you may prefer to leave these off.

Do each row of lace pieces until you feel happy with the result.

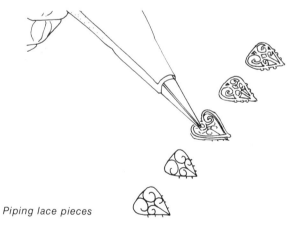

Piping lace pieces

Completed lace pieces may be kept on the lunchwrap in a box until they are needed. An old shirt box can be very useful for this and makes it easier to see which design you have in each box.

To estimate how much lace you will need for your cake measure its circumference and then divide the width of your lace piece into this. Do, however, allow for breakages. The lace should be left to dry for several hours before using; it should then be attached at an angle of 45° but

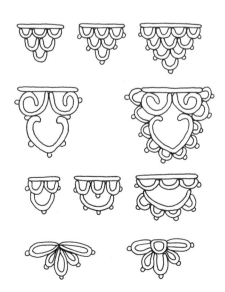

Lace designs

this may not always be possible. Be careful not to make scallop designs too deep if you are going to attach lace, otherwise it will not fit around the curves of the scallops. Remove each piece and attach it to the cake by piping a small line of dots or snail's trail. Do not make this line too long as it will dry off as you are working. The design used for the cake facing page 70 has been included because it gives an alternative use for extension work. These are very fragile pieces due to their extra length. Take note also of the clever use of colours in these laces.

More lace designs

Once you have mastered making lace you may find that it is no longer necessary to use graph paper. Some decorators prefer freehand lace-making for smoother results. See page 135 for more lace patterns.

Extension work

Extension work is sometimes known as 'curtain' or 'bridge' work. It is the extended line work seen at the base of many cakes. Some of the cakes illustrated have double extension work which gives a lovely soft shadow effect when two colours are used. Apricot has been used under the outer layer of white icing of the cake facing page 39. Extension work should not be any deeper than one-third of the depth of the cake, otherwise it looks too heavy. The top of the work can be straight, scalloped, bell or heart shaped. It need not be applied all around the base of the cake; in fact when particular shapes are required it is better to have only small sections of this work . See cake facing page 54 for an example of this style.

The consistency of your icing is the most important part of this work. It should be neither too soft nor too firm; it should be smooth and flow easily from your tube, about the same consistency as for lace work.

Note: If your icing keeps breaking, the reason may be either that you are not pressing firmly and consistently on your cone, or that the icing is too soft. It is very important to have your icing the correct consistency. Or the icing

may be too stiff, in which case add a few drops of water or egg white or, preferably, mix a fresh batch.

A scalloped extension

Step 1
Measure the circumference of the cake, take a piece of greaseproof paper cut to this size, then cut its depth to the required depth for the extension work. Fold this paper as often as you need to make a scallop pattern in the size needed, cut the base in a curve to make the scallops and, depending on whether the top of the extension is to be straight or scalloped, do the same for the top edge of the paper.

Step 2
Pipe a continuous row of beading or snail's trail around the base of the cake where it meets the board. Once this is dry, pin your paper pattern onto the cake so that each scallop base is almost touching the beading. Pin prick this pattern by marking the top and bottom edges of the beginning and base of the scallops. Tubes needed for extension work are No. 00 or No. 000 for the line work and Nos. 1, 2 or 3 for the scallops.

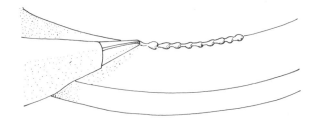

Beading around the base of the cake

Step 3
The first support row is the first row of scallops. Using a No. 1 tube pipe the first row of scallops making sure that none of these accidentally touches the board; each should be placed just above the row of beading. Allow each row to be

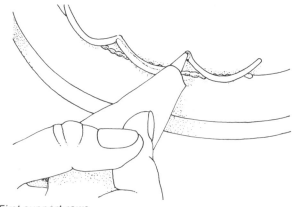

First support rows

perfectly dry before piping the next row on top and continue until you have built up four or five rows of icing. *Adding more rows of icing when the previous one is wet may make the whole lot collapse.*

While these rows are drying you can be doing other embroidery work on the sides of the cake.

Taking a No. 00 tube, start to pipe the vertical lines of the extension work. If you have access to a tilting cake stand, it will allow for easier work. (The cake should lean slightly forward so that the piping lines do not sag in against the cake edge.) The spacing between each line should not be any wider than the width of one strand of icing. The top and bottom of this work may be neatened by attaching lace or by piping a small row of snail's trail along the lower edge. The more experienced decorator may wish to pipe extra support rows over a completed area of extension work and, after building this up to a desirable height, pipe another curtain or layer of vertical strands. Support rows, or bridge rows as they are sometimes known, may be piped in white or contrasting colours. (See facing page 86 for examples of this.)

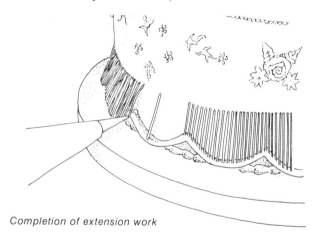

Completion of extension work

Lace carriage

The beautiful miniature carriage between pages 94-95 is made from royal icing. It is piped onto waxed paper and allowed to dry. Then each piece is gently removed and assembled with royal icing. Patterns given allow for two sizes.

Carriage

Step 1
Using a royal icing in the consistency used for lace making, make up an icing bag and insert a tube No. 00 or No. 000. Place a copy of your pattern pieces on a caneite board and then lay a piece of waxed paper over this. Secure with drawing pins. Using the same method as for lines, outline each piece required, including scrolls at base of sides. These lines must be even and straight. If you prefer them thicker, use a No. 0 tube just for this part.

Step 2
Using your finer tube, pipe over the curved inner lines, making sure that each row touches the previous one. This will ensure strength and also allow for easier handling when pieces are dry. Be careful to make the right number of pieces. The less experienced person may wish to make some spares to allow for breakages. Set these aside to dry thoroughly.

Step 3
Pipe the wheels with whichever sized tube you prefer. After they are completely dry, gently peel each wheel off the waxed paper by easing the paper off all the outer edges first. Turn the wheels over and then repipe all the lines again over the previous ones, so that you have a double layer back to back. Set aside to dry thoroughly.

Step 4
Make several pieces of lace in the same way as for lace making. These are needed for the top of the carriage.

Horses

Step 1
Using the pattern given, pipe as many horses as you require, allowing for spares in case of breakages. If your board allows, you may prefer four horses. Two will do just as well. Pipe these outlines in white. Then, using the same method as for floodwork (see page 39), fill in each horse with a softer watered-down icing.

Step 2
Features such as eyes and legs may be piped over when this icing dries. Otherwise use a firmer consistency of icing to allow you to raise these features. Do not forget details such as ears, main and tail. Set these aside to dry thoroughly.

Turn the horses over after they are dry and repeat the process on the other side to give them more body.

Refer to page 41 if you would like to figure pipe your horses. Horses and carriage will have to be assembled directly onto your cake board. Leave them aside until all other items for your cake have been completed.

Horse — make two or four

Side piece — two needed

End piece — two needed

Roof

Base

Wheel — make four

Horse — make two or four

Side piece — two needed

End piece — two needed

Roof

Base

Wheel — make four

Lace carriage

Assembly

Step 1
Pipe a small amount of firm royal icing under each of the horses' feet. Then place them onto the board and support with cotton wool if needed.

Step 2
Pipe another small amount of icing underneath each wheel and attach to the board. Obviously the distance between each wheel will have to be marked out first, using the size of your base piece as a guide. Support the wheels with cotton wool also until these have set firmly.

Step 3
Pipe a running dot line on each piece of the carriage which is to join to another. Do this one section at a time, otherwise your icing will dry too quickly. First secure the base to the two side pieces. Then attach each end piece and finally

place the roof over the top. This carriage is very fragile, so work slowly and carefully. Use a sheet of foam while assembling the carriage to reduce breakages. Support the assembled carriage if necessary and allow to dry.

Step 4
When your carriage is dry, pipe more icing onto the relevant pieces and then gently rest it in place, making sure that it all holds together.

Finally attach pieces of lace to the top of the carriage with a running dot line.

Filigree carriage

Carriage

This is more intricate than the lace carriage. Use a No. 00 or No. 000 writing tube and some royal icing of the same consistency as for the previous carriage.

Step 1
Place the patterns given below on to a caneite board under some waxed paper. Secure with drawing pins and then begin work in the same way as before.

Step 2
Pipe all the outlines first, then outline the inside of the window and door area. Pipe over all the scrolls, ensuring that scrolls are joined where they meet to allow for firm support. If you are using a thicker writing tube, the icing may be too thick to form into scrolls. If this is the case, place dots at these rounded areas to ensure a neat effect.

Step 3
Make two sides, two ends, one base, one roof and four wheels. The wheels for this carriage are a little more fragile, so be careful when you remove them from the waxed paper.

Horses

These may be made in the same way as for the previous carriage. See page 36 for pattern.

Assembly

Assemble in the same way as for the previous carriage. This carriage will not require lace pieces to complete it.

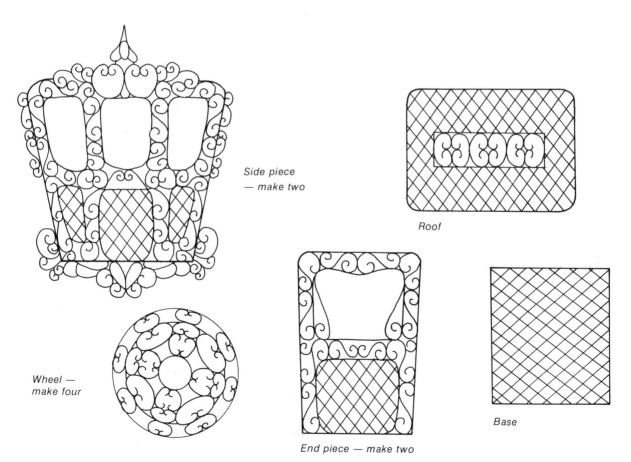

Side piece — make two

Roof

Wheel — make four

End piece — make two

Base

Filigree carriage

Decorated Fairy Cakes

You can either purchase fairy cakes or make some small patty cakes. A large butter cake or sponge may also be used. You can cut this into the required shapes and sizes with fancy cutters.

Make or purchase 250 g of soft icing (also known as plastic icing). You will find recipes for plastic icing on page 129. Gently heat 2-3 tablespoons of sieved apricot jam, add a little water if required. Start with ten fairy cakes. Divide the soft icing into five batches and colour each one differently with a drop or two of colour. Don't add too much colour: soft pastel tones are more acceptable. The colour is worked into the icing by kneading for a short time.

Take the apricot glaze and brush it over the top of each fairy cake. Then take a cutter the size of the cake (or you may cut freehand if you wish) and cut out two pieces from each colour. Place them on the top of each cake so that you have two cakes covered in each of the five icing colours. When you are making more than ten cakes you can use a wider range of colours. Look at facing page 22 for ideas on how to decorate the cakes.

Royal icing is best used for piping on these cakes and any combination of piped flowers and embroidery may be used to add interest. Scale all decorations according to the size of each cake, so that leaves and flowers are neat and small. Practice in this area, including writing names on cakes for children, will be useful for giving you ideas on decorating larger cakes. Marzipan fruits and crystallised flowers used on these cakes are dealt with on pages 43 and 94.

Facing, above: Pansies offer a change in this pretty arrangement made by Mrs Eva Kidd. The maidenhair fern, grape hyacinth and carnations also create an old-world charm, which is complemented by the traditional sugar doily. Note the piped cross stitch near the border.

Facing, below: This elegant sugar plate was made by Mrs Alice Burnham. The lace doily is made from an embroidered piece of icing with a lace edge piped onto the board. Moulded and piped flowers have been used to decorate the plate.

Floodwork, jelly decorating and other decorative ideas

Floodwork

Floodwork (or run-in work) is the art of filling in a picture with royal icing thinned to the right consistency. When doing floodwork, it is advisable to do more than one picture at a time so that, while one section is drying, you can work on another. Also, mixing the colours for fooodwork is extremely time-consuming so you may as well take advantage of having mixed your colours. Floodwork items will keep very well in a strong box protected from dust

There are many methods used in floodwork depending on the effect you want to achieve. Three-dimensional effects are possible by building up several layers of icing, allowing each to dry before adding another. Your picture or design may be outlined first, then filled in with a thinned icing, either by using an icing cone or by applying the icing with a brush. (Sometimes both methods are needed.) Another method is to brush the icing into the picture without having an outline as a guide.

Floodwork may be done straight on to a cake, to a plaque or to waxed paper, then the paper removed and the plaque placed on the cake. The thinned down icing may be left white and coloured later, just as if you were doing a painting. This method may sound a little difficult but it is possible to fill in the picture with coloured icing which, although a little slower (because drying time has to be allowed between each colour) does eliminate the problem of colours running. Any clearly outlined picture is suitable for this type of work,

Facing: There are many features in this cake which make it a beautiful centre-piece for any bridal table. It has a lovely blend of fine hand-moulded flowers, soft embroidery and a moulded umbrella. It was made by Mrs Sue Colclough.

but do start with something simple before going on to a complicated design, such as a scene. Floodwork is an ideal technique to use when decorating a cake for a man, or it makes a lovely gift for a child especially if the painted part can be removed from the cake.

Gum paste or pastillage plaques are included on page 103 with other sugar decorations and ornaments. Plaques may also be made by rolling out fondant icing to a thickness of 3 mm, cutting the required shape and size with a sharp scalpel, and then being set aside to dry. Turn the plaques several times while they are drying so they do not become convex or concave in shape. You may attach the icing to a piece of cardboard by brushing egg white on a cardboard base, then rolling the icing onto this.

If floodwork is required on the side of a cake, the painted pieces may be made separately and attached to the cake with a little royal icing. It can also be applied straight onto the cake but the icing consistency needs to be firmer and the cake should be tilted a little if possible.

Follow the suggestions for this simple piece of floodwork, then you can progress to larger more difficult items once you feel a little more confident.

Step 1

Place the picture to be flooded under a piece of waxed paper. Pin this down onto a caneite board so that it is held firmly in place. Make sure that there are no wrinkles in the paper otherwise the icing will break after it is dry.

We will start with the little dog pictured below. Mix your icing and colour about 125 g of it brown. Fill a cone fitted with a small writing tube with the brown icing. Follow the outlines of the picture. Add a few drops of water to the balance of the brown icing. Put this thinned brown icing into a sharply pointed plain cone. When flooding,

Outlining the picture

keep the end of your cone in the icing and press, filling in the relevant area. If necessary, use your brush to ease the icing up to the outlines of your picture.

First flood the dog's left front and back paws, brushing the icing at the top of each of the legs to taper it away to nothing. Now flood the dog's head, covering the features but making the icing a bit fuller at the nose.

Leave the space for the dog's collar clear. Now flood the dog's body, making the top part of the right back leg of the dog fuller. Do *not* touch any part of the work that has already set.

Flooding the picture

Allow the icing to set and then add the collar in red or yellow — as it is such a small area it is not necessary to thin the icing. Set the dog aside to dry thoroughly and then add the eyes, muzzle and tongue, using either royal icing or painting with food colouring.

If you prefer to fill in the dog with white icing and colour it later, follow the same procedure using white icing until you get to the collar etc. When dry, take some brown food colouring diluted with a little water or methylated spirits and brush over all the relevant areas. With a slightly darker tone, shade in the areas around the legs, paws and ears. These tones will make the dog look more realistic. If the item you are colouring has many shades within it, colour the palest shade first and then highlight other features in a variety of suitable tones. Allow the dog 24 hours to dry before removing from the lunchwrap and attaching to the top of a cake with a few lines of royal icing. Items such as this are very fragile so it is best to make more than one to allow for breakage.

Cartoon characters, the latest pop group or a replica of a birthday card make ideal themes for floodwork. If your design is to be flooded directly onto a cake, trace it on to tracing paper and then redraw onto the surface of the cake by placing the tracing on the top of the cake. Hold it securely in position with some pins placed inside the design, so that no holes will be left on the cake. Trace over this drawing with a pin so that a pin-prick outline is made. After removing the paper continue in the same way as for the dog.

When a fluffy or furry effect is required, instead of using a thin icing, fill in the area with a firmer icing using a star tube, and work over this in the softer icing to give a softer look to the lines created by the star tube.

If you have chosen to do a scene in floodwork, you can achieve a three-dimensional effect. Items in the foreground may be flooded over two or three times to give them different depths. This is done very simply by repeating the flooding-in process as often as required. *Note that the first layer of icing must be completely dry before the second one can be applied.* Sometimes hills or trees in the background are not filled in with icing but are lightly coloured straight onto the cake covering.

This will give a very soft, hazy effect if colour is applied with care. You will see that on the 'Man From Snowy River' cake between pages 30-31 the decorator has used a variety of methods to achieve the final effect. The background hills were coloured with dry chalk while the rest of the work was coloured with liquid food colours.

The illustrations show many styles of floodwork. I hope these will encourage you to try this style of work if you are a beginner. They will also give some inspiration to the more proficient decorator. The illustrations also demonstrate how floodwork may be success-fully combined with any of the other areas of cake decorating.

Flooded butterfly

Take a sheet of waxed paper. Outline the two wings of the butterfly. Flood these in required shades of icing and allow to dry. Pipe the body onto the cake and then with a line of icing gently apply each wing. For more colour and shading see page 125.

Flooded fan

This is a beautiful decoration which can be used for many occasions. Use the template provided as a pattern, and make some spare pieces, because they are very fragile. Do not proceed with pieces that become distorted during drying.

Step 1
Outline as many pieces as you require (12 pieces assemble to a fan large enough for a 20 cm cake). Allow for outlining of holes to thread ribbon through if desired.

Step 2
Flood these pieces in the usual way (see page 39). If you wish to make your fan in a pastel colour, you may use a coloured icing for both the outlining and the flooding. Set these pieces aside to dry.

Step 3
Embroider a pattern over each piece, or just pipe a running dot line around the outer edges. These lines and embroidery may be outlined in gold or silver after they are dry, or the embroidery may be piped in a colour instead. Set aside to dry again.

Step 4
Use a very fine ribbon to assemble the fan. Thread one piece at a time, then gently push each piece into place.

Step 5
When you place the fan on the cake, assemble the base pieces to form a spiral. Smaller flat

flowers and loops of ribbon are suitable to complete the decoration. Attach the end of the ribbon to the underside of the fan with two dots of royal icing.

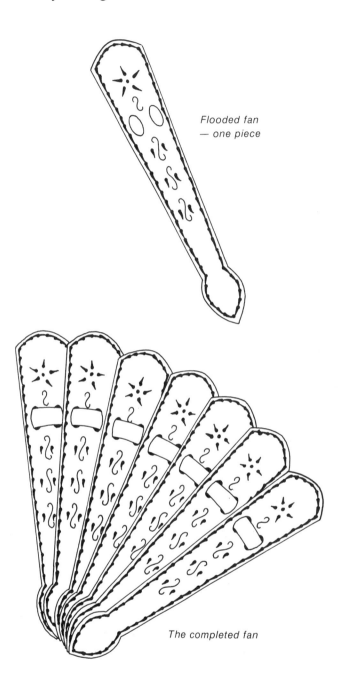

Flooded fan — one piece

The completed fan

Figure piping

This is the art of making free-hand figures, using icing with a little more body. The figures are raised and, in some cases, partly upright. Essentially, if you can draw a stick figure and have proper pressure control of your icing bag, you can do figure piping. It may be done straight onto a cake or the figures may be piped separately and added to the cake afterwards.

Using royal icing made to a consistency that is light but firm enough to hold its shape, take the icing bag with a large hole cut at the end (naturally the size of the hole will depend on the item being made).

Swans

Swans are always lovely, no matter where they are used, and figure piping them is very rewarding. These should be done with white icing.

Step 1

Draw the main outline of a swan on a piece of paper. (See patterns pages 135-139.)

Holding the tube at a 30° angle, press very firmly to get a good globular shape for the head, ease off pressing and move slightly upwards and then downwards to shape the neck.

Swans — Step 1

Step 2

Hold your tube at the base of the swan's neck and press very firmly to make the body. Ease off and taper the icing for the tail.

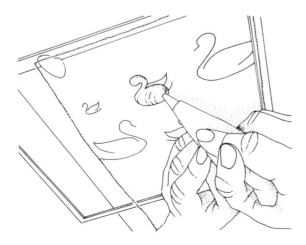

Step 2

Step 3

Pick up your tube and place it against the side of the swan with the top of the tube in the body, press, ease off and then pull away, tapering off for the wing. Using a small writing tube filled with orange royal icing, pipe a beak. When the swan is dry, add a small blue or black dot of royal icing for the eye.

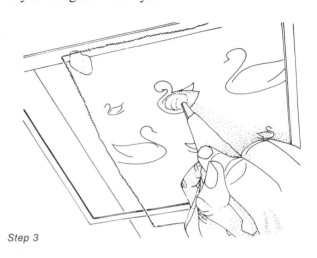

Step 3

If you want your swans to stand upright, turn them over when they are dry and repeat the above procedure on the other side. This can be done for any items made in this way.

You can make different animals, fairies or clowns in this way. The icing can be coloured first. Novelty characters make a good children's party gift or stand them upright on a merry-go-round cake. Make a colourful circus cake with lots of clowns.

Jelly decorating

Decorating with jelly is quick, easy and very effective. Jelly has long been used commercially for writing on cakes but it is now being used in a similar method to flooding. The jelly can be purchased from commercial cake decorating supply stores and is available in plain or in colours. In case you have difficulty obtaining the jelly, I have included a suggested alternative in the recipe section. I find plain jelly is more practical because it can be coloured as required by mixing drops of food colour into small quantities of the jelly. Items made with this jelly do not keep as well as those made with icing but the jelly can still be used weeks ahead. Jelly is suitable for the same sort of designs as floodwork. I find animals and cartoon style pictures look very effective; flowers flooded in this jelly have a bright shiny surface.

Jelly decorating may be used on iced fruit cakes, sponges and small cakes iced in butter or water icing. Because it is so versatile you will find this area of decorating both enjoyable and practical.

Another idea for using jelly technique is to measure the diameter of a sponge (or other suitable cake). Take a small quantity of fondant icing (approx. 250 g), knead this and then roll it out to a thickness of 3 mm. Cut a circular piece using the same measurement as the cake, brush a thin layer of jam over the top of the cake, roll the piece of icing onto your rolling pin and place it on the cake. Ease the icing gently along the edges so that it is smooth and even. This covering may also be used for floodwork. Choose a picture and trace it onto tracing paper and, as with floodwork, pin-prick the drawing onto the icing.

Take 50 g of cooking chocolate and one tablespoon of Copha (or any vegetable shortening). Bring this to body temperature. (Do not overheat otherwise the chocolate will have to be cooled before it can be successfully used for outlining.) Using a paper cone with a writing tube in it, fill the bag with the chocolate but be gentle while closing the cone. Outline your drawing with the chocolate. Keep the tube in a moist cloth while it is not being used otherwise the chocolate will tend to spill out all over your work area. Set aside to cool. Select a variety of food colours to colour jelly. After you have made up a range of colours needed for your design proceed as follows. Fill various cones with different coloured jellies, gently fold the cones and then cut an appropriate size hole in each. Pipe the jelly as required into each section of the design, ensuring that enough jelly is used to allow for complete coverage of each section. In sections requiring shadows or darker tones it is possible to pipe in two or more colours together then blend each tone with your brush.

Use a scrap of icing to test this method before applying it to your design.

Crystallised flowers and fruit

If you don't have time (or feel you have the ability!) to pipe flowers, an inexpensive and easy alternative is to decorate your cake with crystallised flowers or fruit.

How to crystallise

Take one egg white. Whip this to a soft and fluffy, but not stiff, consistency. Use castor sugar, either white or coloured, to match the flower. If food colouring is used to colour the sugar, either allow the sugar to dry overnight or place it on a flat tray and leave in a cool oven just long enough to dry off the moisture. Using a medium size brush, gently but thoroughly coat the flower all over with egg white. Ensure that the petals, calyx, centre and stem (if required) are all covered with egg. Make sure that the back of the flower is also treated and that each petal is individually coated. Sprinkle the flower with castor sugar, again making sure that every surface is covered. *Do not dip the flower into the sugar;* the weight of sugar will make the flower droop. Shake off any excess sugar and place flowers onto paper towelling or a fine wire rack to dry thoroughly. If your flower looks droopy after this treatment, rearrange the petals and gently support with toothpicks until dry. The flowers will improve in appearance once they are dry. Any flowers with firm petals are suitable for crystallising; violets, small roses, daisies or jonquils can all look beautiful. Small items of fruit are also very attractive. There are four important points to remember about crystallising:

- if too much egg white is used, your flowers will droop and fall apart
- it can take several days for crystallised items to dry completely
- crystallised flowers become very brittle when they are dry and petals may break off easily
- do not eat crystallised flowers unless you are certain that they have no toxic ingredients.

You can store crystallised flowers for six months or longer, so flowers which are out of season can be used at any time. Store them in a cardboard box or airtight jar; they will not keep in plastic containers, as moisture builds up. Silica gel crystals should be used to absorb excess moisture from stored crystallised flowers, especially during humid conditions.

Decorated Easter eggs

Personalised eggs are easy, inexpensive and fun to create. Although you can make chocolate eggs, I have only given directions for sugar eggs as they are easier to handle and store. You can buy commercially-made chocolate eggs and decorate them in the same way as sugar eggs. Either smooth or rippled surfaces are suitable.

Sugar eggs may be made by two methods. (The same applies to sugar bells, page 100.) Egg moulds are available of wood, plaster or plastic; any is suitable. Or use an animal- or shell-shaped mould or shells.

Basic eggs

Method 1

Step 1
Make up a batch of moulding sugar by mixing 1 kg of castor sugar with one egg white. If you wish, add a few drops of food colouring to this mixture. Press the sugar gently but firmly; but don't pack the sugar in too hard as this makes it difficult to remove from the mould. Level off the sugar with a knife. This must be done, as the egg will crack if the surface of the sugar is left uneven.

Step 2
Place a piece of firm board, glass or cardboard over the mould; turn the mould over immediately and gently remove it. Then fill and turn out the second half of the egg.

Step 3
Dry eggs at room temperature, or for speed, turn out onto a wooden board and place in an oven 180° C (350° F) for five minutes. If you are drying your eggs in the oven, make only one pair at a time or your sugar will dry out too quickly.

Step 4
When dry, hold the egg gently and begin to hollow it out. Be careful not to shatter the egg while it is still warm, although it is easier to scoop out the inside sugar while it is a little warm. Make your egg as thick or as fine as you wish; the sugar that has been scooped out can be reused. (If it becomes too dry, add a few drops

of water to moisten it again.) Join the two halves by piping a line of royal icing along the outside edge and pressing them together.

Step 5
You can leave your egg with an open front, with a scene or novelties arranged inside. Make one half in the normal way and set aside. Take the other half of the egg and, about a third of the way down, pull a tautly held length of cotton halfway across the egg.

Step 6
Slide the thread out sideways, then repeat this procedure from the other side so that you have sliced right across the egg, but do not remove this upper section.

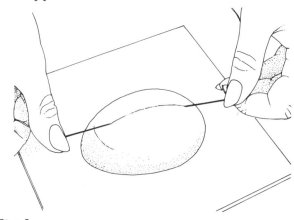

Step 6

Step 7
Leave this half and the other half to set.

Step 8
Remove the upper section while scooping the second half of the egg as this will prevent it from collapsing while it is drying. Join the two halves as before. You can either sit the egg on top of a circle of firm cardboard or use a sugar bell as a stand. Bells are made in the same way as eggs but are scooped out from the bottom.

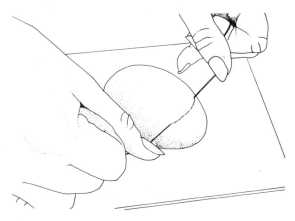

Slicing egg — Step 5

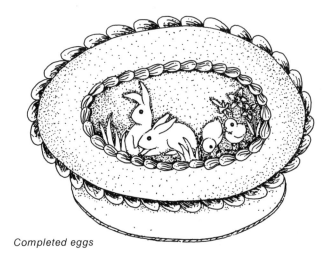

Completed eggs

Method 2

Step 1

Take 500 g of soft icing. Colour with food colouring if required and add one teaspoon of Tragacanth gum powder if you want your eggs to dry quickly. This gum is available from chemists and, although expensive, it is convenient to use, especially in humid climates.

Step 2

Roll out the icing to the desired thickness — 4 mm is a good thickness. Put cornflour in your mould so that the icing will not stick, and gently press the icing into the shape. Press firmly, but gently, with an even pressure so that the egg remains the same thickness all over.

Step 3

Cut away any excess icing; test and loosen the edges gently to ensure that the icing will slide out of the mould when it is dry.

Step 4

Leave in the mould for thirty minutes to retain the shape, then turn onto a board and allow to dry. Join the halves as described in Method 1.

Decorating ideas

Arrange sprays of piped flowers across the front of the eggs, using a small dob of royal icing to attach them. Leaves, embroidery and a name may be piped to complete the arrangement.

Piped Easter egg

Using two halves left open at one end (attach one half about half-way down the length of the other so as to give the impression of an open chest) decorate the outer part of the egg with royal icing to resemble a treasure chest. The chest may be filled with small eggs or sweets.

Treasure chest

A doll's cradle may be made by using one half egg-shape and one quarter. Attach the quarter so as to form the 'hood'. Place two small lengths of rolled icing, one at each end, to make a stand. The outside of the cradle may be decorated with basketweave piping to give the impression of a wicker cradle. Place a small piece of tulle on each side of the cradle and attach with a small cluster of flowers. Finally, place a small sugar baby or doll inside and cover with a blanket made of icing.

Doll's cradle

Other ideas for decorating Easter eggs are nursery rhyme characters, clowns or animals. All sorts of decorative features can be made from scraps of left-over icing: hats, eyes, collars, ears etc, can be piped directly onto the egg in the appropriate colours.

Examples of decorated Easter eggs can be seen between pages 126-127.

Flower moulding

Flower moulding

There are thousands of different flowers and, in some cases, hundreds of different types of one flower (for example, the orchid), so the flowers given here are only those most suitable for cake decorating. There are, of course, many more that can be made in icing and the techniques given here may be used no matter what flower is made — a study of real flowers will reveal that there is no limit to the variety you can make.

If you do this you will also see that there is nearly always more than one shade in each petal. Consequently your shading will determine the degree to which your flowers look realistic. Food colouring applied to your moulding paste with a paintbrush can result in remarkable effects.

I have started with very simple flowers to enable you to master the basic techniques.

Flower cutters or cardboard templates may be used for making flowers; or they may be made freehand. Most decorators use a variety of methods depending on the flower being made.

Various plastic or wooden modelling tools available at art and craft shops can also be used for moulding flowers.

Equipment items needed for this work are listed on page 1. If you do not have any of these items, or prefer to improvise, you can usually adapt the directions to your needs. Some gum paste recipes are provided in the recipes (page 129). The recipe I prefer is the first one listed. Your choice of recipe can be influenced by differing climatic conditions, availability of particular ingredients, and the cost of the sort of work you are doing. The characteristics of each paste are described with the recipes.

I prefer to use white gum paste and colour each flower after it is dry. The gum paste may, however, be coloured in a pale shade of the colour needed and then shaded further as required. You colour gum paste by kneading a drop or two of colour into the paste. Ensure that the colour is worked thoroughly into the gum paste otherwise you will have a streaky effect.

Gum paste dries very quickly so do not make up a large quantity. Do not allow it to remain uncovered while not in use. Put all excess gum paste in a small plastic bag to ensure it remains soft and pliable. If several petals or leaves are to be cut at the one time, cover them with a glass or plastic lid until they are ready to be used.

Directions for flowers are listed in three categories.
- *Large flowers*   Included in this list are some basic flowers which are very popular and easy to make.
- *Small or medium flowers*   This section includes many of the flowers used on the cakes in this book.
- *Flowers native to Australia*   Many examples are given although it would be impossible to include them all.

Briar rose

Briar roses may be made either using cutters or freehand. They are a very popular and versatile flower and are suitable for cakes for any occasion. These flowers may be made in single or double form.

Flower

Method 1

Step 1
Take a ball of gum paste which is firm and pliable, neither too dry nor too soft. (This consistency is needed for all flower-making unless otherwise stated.) Place excess paste into

a plastic bag. Pull a small piece of paste away from the ball; work it to a fine smooth petal of the required size, then break it off the ball and and smooth the base edges.

Step 2
Place the petal in the palm of the left hand and bend your fingers forward over the top edge of the petal to flute the edge. Do not close your hand too far over the petal or you will squash it. Place the petal into a foil-lined patty tin (the shallow variety is best).

Step 3
Make five petals like this. As you make them attach them to each other. With a paintbrush, paint a little egg white or water onto a section of the right-hand edge of the first petal. Repeat the procedure for the second petal and attach it to the first petal, overlapping it by about 5 mm.

Continue adding the petals in this way, tucking the right-hand side of the last petal under the edge of the first petal. If the patty tin does not support the flower once it is assembled, pleat a piece of foil to allow it to take up the shape required.

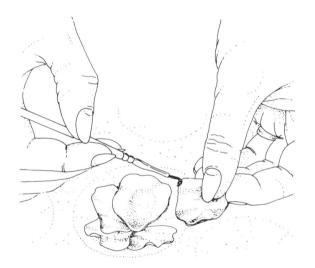

Method 1 — Step 3

Step 4
The centre of the flower is made by piping some firm royal icing into the centre space. To finish off, take a number of stamens and cut these to approximately 5 mm in length. Briar roses have many stamens; to give a more realistic look your stamens may be curved gently and some placed in deeper than others. Using tweezers, place them one by one on the outer edges of the royal icing centre. Both the flower and stamens may be coloured either at this stage or later when you are assembling a spray (see page 122).

Step 4

Method 2
Take a briar rose cutter. If you use a variety of sizes, you will be able to make a graded selection of flowers, as well as some double flowers. If cutters are unavailable, use these patterns to make a set of templates.

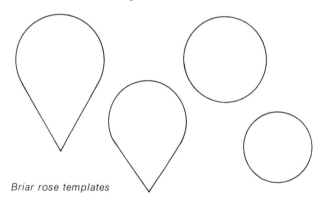

Briar rose templates

Step 1
Using your small rolling pin, roll out a small quantity of gum paste and, using the cutter you have selected, cut out five petals. Place any left-over paste with the balance of your paste in the plastic bag. Pick up one of the petals and cover the others with a glass or plastic lid.

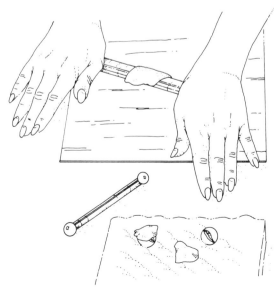

Method 2 — Step 1

Step 2
Place the petal on your left hand with the round edge of the petal away from the palm. With the end of your paint brush or a rounded skewer, press firmly around the edge of the petal to thin and flute it slightly.

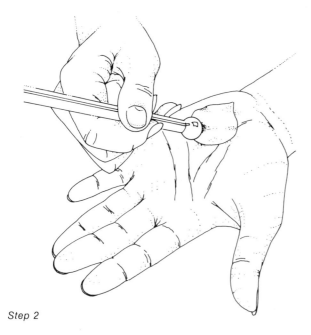

Step 2

Place this into a patty tin and proceed as in Method 1. You can press each petal into a piece of foam rubber to curve the petals, then arrange into a flower as described in Method 1.

Step 3
Form a large dot of royal icing and arrange the petals into this. Overlap in the same way as described in Method 1. Finish by adding stamens to the centre. Allow to dry for 24 hours before peeling the flowers off the foil.

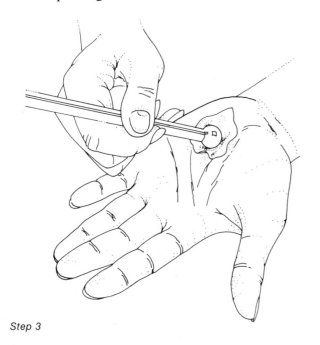

Step 3

Alternative centre for briar rose

Step 1
Break off some paste about half the size of a pea and work it a little with your fingers. Roll it into a ball then flatten it slightly against some tulle or net.

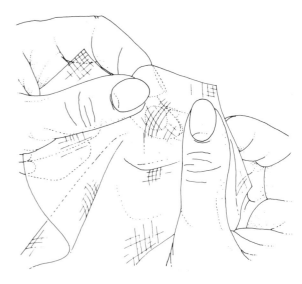

Centre of the briar rose — Step 1

Step 2
Cut 5 mm off each end of a number of stamens and push them into the paste centre all around the edge about 1 mm apart, curving them slightly upwards.

Paint a little egg white into the centre of the petals and attach the centre with the stamens.

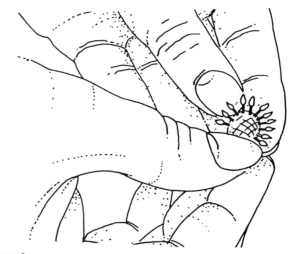

Step 2

Leaves

The leaves described below are not necessarily only for briar roses. The method used for making leaves is the same for most flowers. The shape, length and colour is altered to suit each variety. Although the colour scheme for most cakes will be in pale pastel shades a touch of greenery is often a welcome contrast.

You can either cut your leaves freehand or use a plain or serrated-edge leaf cutter or a plastic leaf.

Step 1
Plastic leaves: may be used individually. Cut them from the stem of a plastic rose and cover the veined surface with cornflour. Using either a rolling pin or your hands, flatten a small piece of gum paste, ensuring that it is large enough to cover the surface of the cornflour-coated leaf. Press the paste gently over all the veined area, then cut away the edges of the leaf, pulling off any excess paste.

Step 2
Allow the leaf to set for a couple of minutes and then gently peel away the plastic leaf.

Step 3
Arrange these leaves to dry in a variety of shapes with slight bends or twists, or lay some over the handle of a wooden spoon so that a natural looking curve is achieved.

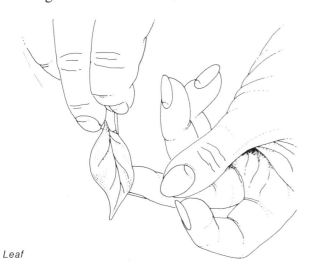

Leaf

Step 1
Freehand leaves: Roll out some gum paste to the desired thickness and then cut out your leaves by using your scalpel or art knife.

Step 2
Using the back of your blade, indent a veined pattern and form serrated edges by gently pressing the tip of the blade at regular intervals on the outside edge of the paste.

Step 3
If your leaves are to be wired, take a piece of cotton-covered wire and form a small hook at the end. Moisten with a touch of water and then insert this hooked end into the base of the leaf. Ease this wire into the paste gently otherwise it will break the leaf. Pinch the leaf at the base to ensure that it is held in position firmly. Ensure that your fingers are well covered with cornflour before pinching the leaf to avoid excess moisture problems.

Leaves on roses are usually arranged in clusters of three. Don't forget to make your leaves in graded sizes like your flowers, to give the most natural appearance possible. Refer to page 125 for suggestions on colouring of flowers, leaves and buds. Instructions for taping and wiring sprays of flowers are given on page 122.

Buds

The bud for the briar rose can be made in two or three ways, to allow for grading when forming a spray.

Method 1

Step 1
Take a small piece of gum paste and shape this into a bullet shape or an elongated cone shape.

Step 2
Form a small hook on a piece of cotton-covered wire, moisten with water and insert into the shape. Ease the gum paste around the wire so that it does not fall off.

Method 2

Step 1
Take a small piece of gum paste, flatten it around the edges with the fingers but leave a small fat area at one end.

Step 2
Moisten the flattened edges with a little water and roll this section over and around the fat centre. This will give the impression of a small bud about to open, with the first petal unfurling.

Step 3
Cut off any excess paste from the base and insert wire as in Method 1.

A calyx may be attached separately to these buds (see page 50) or it may be painted on once the buds have dried.

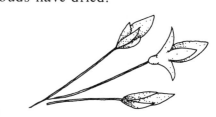

Buds

Calyx

Most flowers have a calyx that supports the petals, though in cake decorating not all flowers are made with a calyx, even if they have one in their natural form. You can choose whether or not to make a calyx for your flowers, although I recommend that you do so for show work. A calyx makes it easier both to assemble a spray of flowers and to arrange the flowers on your cake.

Directions on how to make a calyx for the briar rose are given below. This is a fairly common type of calyx and the same method will be used for many varieties of flowers. Do, however, look at real flowers to see the exact size and number of sepals needed for each variety of flower that you make.

Step 1
Take a piece of gum paste about the size of a pea. Using the end of your paint brush or rounded skewer, insert it into the centre of the ball and press outwards. Rotate the brush in a clockwise motion so that a cone shape is formed.

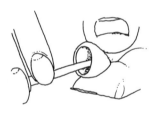

Briar rose calyx — Step 1

Step 2
When this cone is of the required thickness, cut five evenly spaced slits to about half the depth of the cone. Use small scissors for this.

Step 2

Step 3
Take each section and cut to form a pointed sepal. Mitre each sepal by fingering to the required thickness and length.

Step 3

Step 4
Moisten the inside of the calyx. Place a completed dried flower onto a piece of cotton wool, bottom side up.

Step 5
Place the calyx onto the centre of the base of the flower. Press gently along the length of the sepals to allow them to stick onto the flower.

Step 5

Step 6
Insert a piece of hooked wire into the base of the calyx. Press firmly to ensure that the wire remains attached, then leave the whole flower to dry.

Blossom

Blossom is a versatile flower which can be made in many colours and sizes. There are illustrations of blossoms facing pages 86 and 87.

Flower

Method 1

Step 1
With a blossom cutter or with your scalpel cut out five petals from a piece of gum paste which has been rolled out thinly. It is best to keep your piece of gum paste moving while rolling it out so that it does not stick to your tile. Keep your tile lightly dusted with cornflour but do not use too much cornflour or the paste will dry and crack very easily. This can also be a problem during very hot or draughty conditions.

Blossom petal template

Step 2
Cover four of the petals with a lid and, using the same method as for the briar rose, place one petal in the left hand; flute and frill the top rounded edge of the petal by stretching the paste with your paint brush handle. If you prefer a more 'tailored' looking flower, the base may be pinched on the underside and the petal curved

only at the top by pressing it into foam rubber or gently curving over with your thumb.

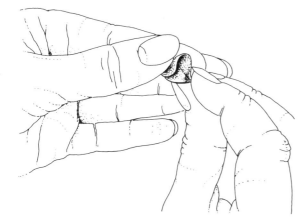

Blossom flower — Step 1

Step 3

Place the petal in a foil-lined patty tin while you work on the rest of the petals. Allow these to dry before assembling.

Step 4

Pipe a large dot of royal icing into the centre of one of the pieces of foil. Place the five petals into this icing and arrange them as for the briar rose. Petals may overlap in the same way. Some blossoms have many stamens while others have only five. The length of these will be determined by your own requirements. Curve them and insert into the icing one at a time. Leave the flowers to set thoroughly. Once set, press gently underneath the foil to remove the flower — store the flowers in a box until needed.

If you prefer to make flowers not quite so open, raise the petals slightly and either support with cotton wool or pinch the foil into the required shape and size. A calyx may be attached.

Buds are made in a more rounded shape but the method is the same as for the bullet shaped briar rose bud. Naturally these buds should be smaller.

Make leaves if required but again style them to blend with the size and type of blossom.

Method 2

Another method used for making blossoms is to use a cutter which cuts the entire flower in one piece, as illustrated below.

Blossom cutter

Roll out a piece of paste to the required thickness and cut out several flowers. Press each into a piece of foam. (The rounded end of a hair curler pin will enable you to achieve a cup effect instead of damaging the petal by using your fingers.) Set aside to dry, then either pipe a little royal icing into the centre to attach your stamens or insert them a little way into the paste.

Completed blossom flower

Frangipani

I use three sizes for frangipani cutters, though the middle size is the one I use the most. Sometimes a combination of sizes can be used to give a realistic look to an arrangement. The first method does not require cottons.

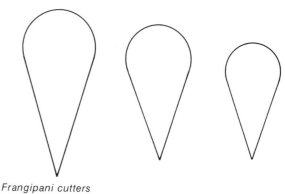

Frangipani cutters

Flower

Method 1

Step 1

Work up a piece of gum paste to the required consistency. Pull a piece up from the ball of paste; it will need to be as long as the length of the largest cutter. Work this piece to a curved shape at the top. Fine petals are much more realistic than thick ones.

Use the movement of your thumb along the inside of this petal to smooth out the gum paste. This will also help create a curved, rolled edge on the left of the petal.

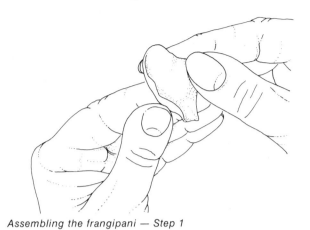

Assembling the frangipani — Step 1

Step 2
Pull on the petal, shape the base to a point and lay it curved on the top of the patty tin.

Step 3
Make five petals like this, of even texture and of equal length.

Step 4
Take one petal in your hand. Moisten the lower half of the right-hand edge with a brush using water or egg white. Lay the left-hand edge of the second petal over the moistened first petal so that they overlap about 5 mm. Repeat with all the petals.

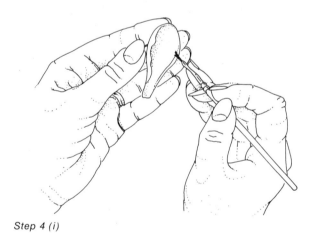

Step 4 (i)

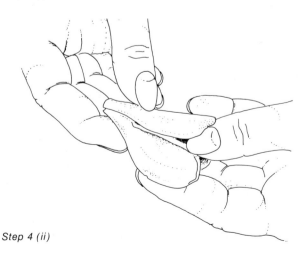

Step 4 (ii)

Step 5
Place the moistened edge of the fifth petal under the left-hand side of the first petal so that you create a cone at the base of the flower.

Step 6
Firm this base between the fingers so that all the petals are attached firmly and you have made a neat, firm point at the base of the flower. Take an empty egg carton, turn it upside down and cut a hole in the base. Insert the flower into this carton and gently ease the petals with the handle of your paint brush to space them evenly. You can also curve them over a little but not if the flower is too dry as it will crack. This method is best to produce large open flower. (A deep bottle top or a narrow necked bottle may be used instead of the egg carton.)

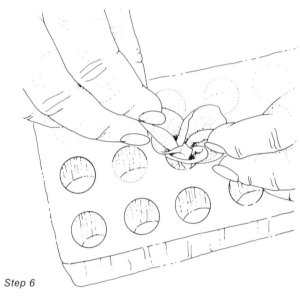

Step 6

Method 2

Step 1
Roll out a small piece of gum paste and cut five petals with one of the frangipani petal shapes. Pick up one petal, covering the other four with a lid.

Hold the petal facing you in your left hand between thumb and forefinger. Roll and unroll the edge of the petal with your thumb to get the correct edge. This takes some practice but you will master it very quickly if you keep trying.

Step 2
Place the petal with the rolled edge lengthwise over the handle of a wooden spoon to curve the petal. Prepare the other four petals in the same way and place each one over the narrow part of the previous one to prevent it drying out too quickly. Leave the last petal to dry for a few minutes.

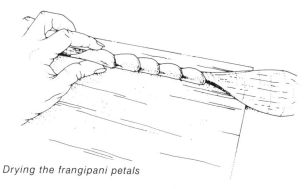

Drying the frangipani petals

Step 3

Place the first petal (which should be pliable) on your tile and paint a little egg white on its lower right-hand edge. Put the second petal onto the edge of the first one and paint its right-hand edge in turn with egg white. Continue in this way adding all the petals to form a fan.

Step 4

After painting egg white on the right-hand edge of the last petal, using a small flat knife, pick up and roll the petals to join them together into a cylinder. Press the base of the petals together and twist slightly. If necessary, cut off any excess paste at the base.

Place the flower in a hole in an egg carton as in Method 1. Using the back of your paint brush and your fingers, gently space the petals evenly and curve them slightly outwards. For variety, some flowers may be left slightly closed.

The frangipani does not have a true calyx so no calyx is necessary.

Bud

Roll a piece of paste into a ball the size of a very large pea. Now roll this ball into a cylinder tapering slightly at each end.

Then, using a smooth-bladed knife, mark five lines around the cylinder. Finally, twist the cylinder slightly so that the lines appear to curve around it.

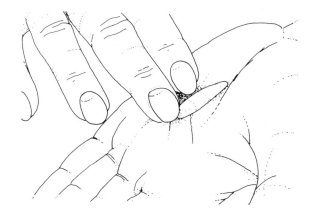

Frangipani bud — Step 1

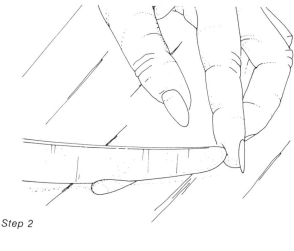

Step 2

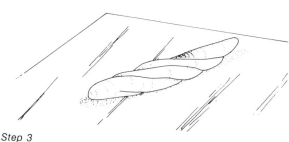

Step 3

Leaf

The real frangipani leaf is very large compared to the flower. In cake decorating, it has to be made smaller than life-size and is cut free-hand. Mark the veins on the leaf with the back of the scalpel blade and set it aside to dry.

Roses

Roses are always a favourite in cake decorating, and because there are so many varieties and sizes, you can choose the most suitable type for any occasion. Instructions for three varieties are given below.

Miniature rose

The miniature rose is ideal for use as a specimen flower. It is the best rose for wiring as it is so small and compact. See facing page 55 for an example of miniature roses used in a floral arrangement suitabe for a table centre.

Rose cones

Step 1

Take a piece of covered wire 75-100 mm long. Bend over 2-3 mm at one end. Dip the curved end of the wire into egg white and then push it into the centre of a pea-sized piece of paste. Shape this piece of paste into a cone 20 mm long and then push the other end of the wire into a piece of Oasis or similar material to allow the cone to dry thoroughly.

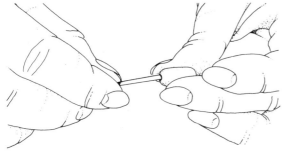

Inserting the wire

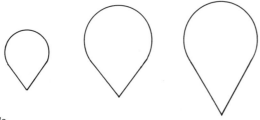

The shaped rose cone

Step 2
Roll out the paste and cut five second or third size briar rose petals.

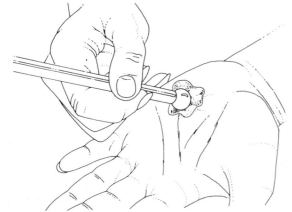

Petals

Step 3
Using your paint brush handle, gently thin the round edge of the first petal.

Hollowing out the petal — Step 4

Step 4
Very slightly hollow out the petal with the end of a rounded skewer and put the petal aside. Repeat this with the next four petals, intensifying the fluting and hollowing for each successive one.

Step 5
Paint a little egg white on each side of the lower point and down the centre of the first petal.

Step 5

Step 6
Wrap this petal around the cone so that the latter does not show.

Step 6

Step 7
Paint egg white onto either side of the lower point of the second petal. Attach the petal to the cone, overlapping the first petal, and wrap it around the cone.

Facing: This cake is very simple, but has a beautiful arrangement of early spring flowers. Mrs Rose Whitehead has presented daffodils, daphne, boronia and freesias to achieve a beautiful but unusual wedding cake set on a mirror base.

Top: An unusual presentation of sweet peas and lily of the valley has been used by Mrs Margaret McGann in this spray. This idea will be of great assistance for the graceful presentation of moulded flowers.

Below and inset: This diamond-shaped arrangement of finely moulded flowers, made by Mrs Dorothy Silva, has grace and elegance. The four varieties of flowers — carnations, roses, jasmine and gypsophila — are all miniatures, in keeping with the size of the arrangement.

Mrs Pam Leman has achieved a beautiful blend of colours in this plaque, which features gardenias, hyacinths, bouvardia, lilac, violets and variegated ivy leaves against a green velvet background.

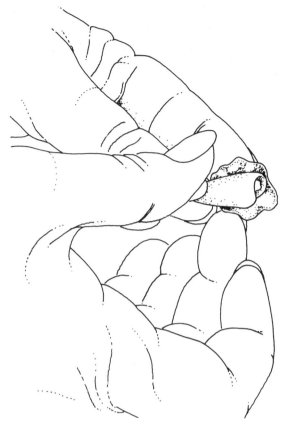

Step 7

Step 8
Paint egg white onto either side of the lower points of the third, fourth and fifth petals; attach the third petal to the cone on the side over the edge of the second one.

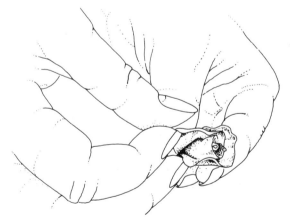

Step 8

Facing page
Above left: This hand-made sugar egg by Mrs Marilyn Lock skilfully combines floodwork and moulded flowers.

Above right: This hand-made chocolate Easter egg by Mrs Maureen Gates contains chickens made of sugar. Note the fragile lacework and the delicately worked roses and boronia.

Below: Mrs Rena Hurtado has used delicate two-toned lacework in the shape of flowers and unusual pink daisies to decorate this chocolate Easter egg.

Step 9
Attach the fourth petal to the other side of the cone, slightly overlapping the third.

Step 10
Attach the fifth petal, tucking it in under the third one. Curve back the petal edges slightly. Set the rose aside to dry, but before completing the flower, make a few roses to this stage of the process.

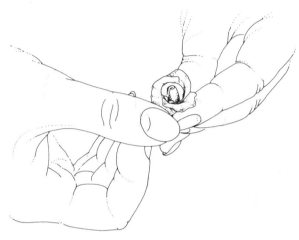

Step 10

Step 11
For the next set of petals, cut three or four more petals with the same size cutter. Flute and hollow them as you did the third, fourth and fifth petals and attach them to the cone in the same way, but overlapping the petals around the cone, and curving the top edges of the petals slightly more, tucking the last of these petals under the first one. Allow the rose to dry.

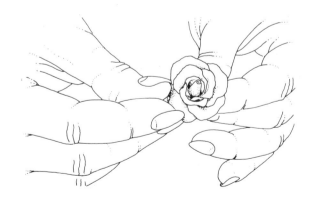

Step 11

Calyx

Step 1
Roll and cut (with a cutter) a rose calyx from some gum paste.

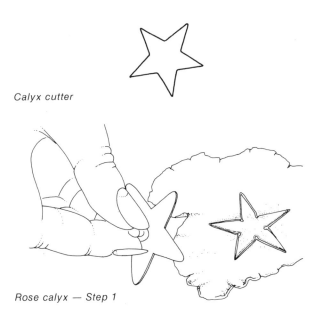

Calyx cutter

Rose calyx — Step 1

Step 2
Turn the calyx over and place it on the palm of your left hand. Move the small rounded end of a skewer from the end of each sepal to its centre and then hollow out the centre of the calyx. Pinch the ends of each sepal to make sharp points.

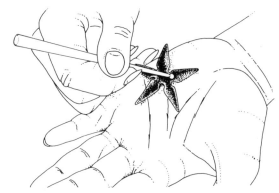

Step 2

Step 3
Using your small scissors, cut a tiny strip away from the base of each sepal.

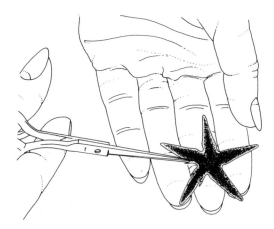

Step 3

Step 4
Turn the calyx over and paint egg white onto its centre and a little way along each sepal.

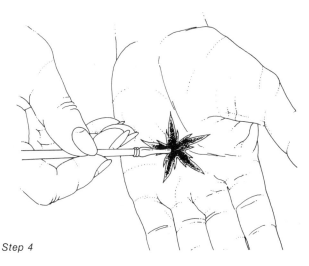

Step 4

Step 5
Join the calyx to the rose by pushing a wire stem through the centre of the rose and then the calyx.

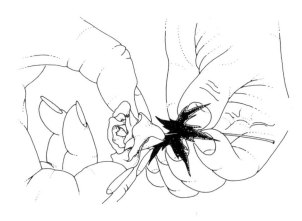

Step 5

Step 6
Roll some gum paste into a ball the size of a small pea. Flatten one side slightly, paint that side with egg white and push the wire stem through the ball, flat side uppermost, to form the hip of the rose.

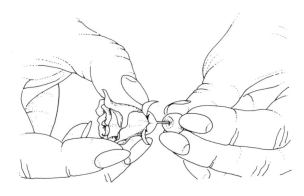

Step 6

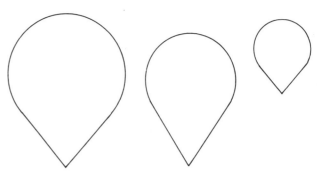

Rose petal cutters

Step 7
Gently curve back the sepals of the calyx and set rose and calyx aside to dry thoroughly.

Step 7

Note: The method described above for making the calyx is most suitable for specimen flowers.

When you need a large number of roses on a cake, it is not always practical to do it in this way; you can leave the sepals of the calyx flat against the rose on one side and not cut the little side pieces on each sepal. The reason for this is that the dry calyx is very brittle and any folded back or jutting out sepals might break off. Fold back the one or two sepals that would be uppermost, not touching the cake or other flowers.

Bud
The rose bud is made in exactly the same way as the rose but is complete after the fifth petal has been attached. Add the calyx and hip, leaving the sepals of the calyx against the bud.

Leaf
Rose leaves are usually in groups of five on a stem, but this is not always practicable. You may wish to use the same method and number of leaves as for the briar rose.

Full blown rose
Some beautiful examples of full blown roses are shown facing page 77. These roses may be moulded freehand or with a three-size set of cutters or templates. Full roses are not usually wired, so they do not need a calyx. You will, however, need stamens for their centres. Your flowers should have an odd number of petals but as you need to have enough petals to give a realistic effect, you may find that some flowers have more petals than others.

Flower
The petals for this rose are made in the same way as for the miniature rose, but are larger. See illustrations above as a guide.

Step 1
Take a piece of paste and roll it out to a fine thickness. Using your smallest cutter, cut out three petals and cover the remaining paste with a lid.

Step 2
Using your brush handle stretch the outer edges of your petals to flute them.

Step 3
Moisten the base and lower right-hand edge of your first petal. Lay the second petal over the first one so that one-third of the petal is overlapping. Do not moisten your petals too far up as they will not look open enough. Continue in this way with the first three petals and fold them in a little.

Step 4
If you wish, pipe a small amount of royal icing into the base of the centre you have formed and insert six to eight stamens into this icing. The length of your stamens should be as high as the petals; you may curve them to achieve a realistic effect.

Step 5
Using your next size cutter, roll out another piece of paste and cut out five petals. Cover the remaining paste and the petals that you are not working with.

Step 6
Taking one petal at a time stretch, flute and vein them. Moisten the bases and lower right-hand edges and attach to the centre you have already made. Allow each petal to appear slightly more open than the previous one. The top edges of these petals are curved out from the centre of the flower by rolling and pinching between the

thumb and forefinger. Support each petal with your left hand while you do this.

Step 7
If your petals fall out of shape, stiffen your paste a little. I find that my outer petals are much stiffer and dryer than the inner ones while I am working. Petals may also be made, shaped, and allowed to dry shortly before assembling to ensure a good shape.

If you are a beginner and find this method too difficult, try making all your petals first. Allow them to dry but support each petal with foil or cotton wool to hold their shape.

Step 8
Using a foil-lined patty tin assemble your flower with some stiff royal icing. Start with the centre: pipe a large dot and then assemble the first three petals.

Step 9
Add your stamens using a pair of tweezers, then continue with your next five petals (or as many more as you need).

Use your medium and large cutter for your second and third layer of petals. Allow to dry completely before you peel your flower off from the foil.

If these two methods of assembly do not help, make your first petal freehand and allow a medium piece of paste to remain at the base of this petal. Press the excess paste down on the flat surface you are working on so that it forms a base into which you can attach petals. Moisten each petal and attach as described in the first method. In this case, however, each petal is attached to the base stem or stand of excess paste.

When your flower is complete cut off this excess base with a sharp knife and allow to dry thoroughly.

Bud

See other rose instructions on page 53.

Calyx

This is not usually needed on large roses. However, see instructions on page 55 if necessary.

Cecil Brunner roses

This rose is one of the most popular flowers used in cake decorating because of its dainty size; it has been used on the cakes facing pages 39 and 86.

You can also make this rose successfully on the side of a cake. The most common form used is an open bud. It appears only to have seven petals, though in fact there are many more petals tightly packed into the central bud of the flower.

Flower

Step 1
Take a small piece of paste the size of a pea. Using your hands only, flatten this piece out to form a small rounded petal with a flat bubble at the base.

Step 2
Roll the thinned out part of the petal around the fat part thus giving the impression of a full bud. Moisten the inner edge so that it remains in place.

Step 3
Make three petals. You may mould these freehand or use a small rose cutter if you prefer.

Cecil Brunner rose petals

Step 4
The first row of petals is wrapped around the centre bud. After completing each petal, moisten the lower edges and wrap around the bud. Make sure that each petal partly overlaps the previous one. Flowers made to this stage are needed as well as the full flower; they can be completed by twisting the base of the flower between the thumb and fore finger to remove excess paste.

Step 5
For the fuller flower proceed one step further. Make three more petals, a little larger than the previous three. This time the outer edges of the petals may be fluted and stretched to give a finer appearance. Veining may be added by pressing each petal over a plastic petal which has vein marks or by pressing into the centre of the hand. Flute the outer edges with the handle of a paint brush.

Step 6
Moisten the outer lower edges to attach the petal. Pinch each petal a little and fold back so that the petal almost appears to be pointed at its top centre. Overlap each petal as you attach it.

Neaten the base by pinching off excess paste. Depending on where these flowers will be placed on your cake, you may wish to make calyxes and wire them, or you may make a pointed calyx with no wire attached. These flowers may be left to dry either in an upturned egg carton or with the wire pressed into a piece of Oasis.

Bud

The buds for this flower can be made by making only the central petal, then neatening off the base. Others may be made to the first row of petals.

Calyx

A calyx for this flower is made in the same way as for the larger rose (but scaled to a suitable size).

Fuchsia

There are many flowers that have several varieties: large, small, single, or double and in a multitude of colours. The fuchsia is one of these. A basic method for fuchsia is given which you may adapt to suit your needs.

Flower

Step 1
Roll some white paste into a ball a little smaller than a marble. Push a rounded skewer firmly into the paste. Shape it over the skewer, constantly moving the paste to prevent it sticking, and hollow it out into a fairly long bell shape.

Step 2
Remove the paste from the skewer and thin it evenly all round with your fingers. Using a pair of small scissors, cut four deep, evenly spaced slits in this shape and then form each section into a petal.

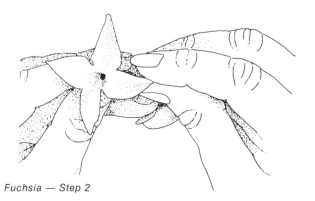

Fuchsia — Step 2

Step 3
Cut away the excess paste working from the centre of each of the four parts, and shape each into a point. Gently fold back these petals and then again hollow out the bell shape, keeping the back long and narrow. Pinch the point of each petal to make it sharper. Set aside gently to dry with the open part upwards.

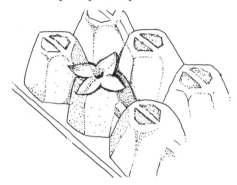

Step 3

Step 4
Roll out some more paste very thinly and cut four petals with a small rose petal cutter. Place a petal on your hand and with the handle of your paint brush, thin and flute the rounded part of each petal.

Step 5
Hollow out each petal slightly. Paint egg white onto the lower right-hand edge of each petal, attach the petals to one another to form a fan shape and then join the end petals to form a cone.

Step 5

Step 6
Paint egg white into the bell shape and stick the cone of petals into it. Push in the petals with the back of your paint brush. Cut six yellow stamens 30 mm long and one 50 mm long. Paint

more egg white into the centre of the petals and then insert the stamens. Stand the flower in an upturned egg carton with the petals upwards until properly dry.

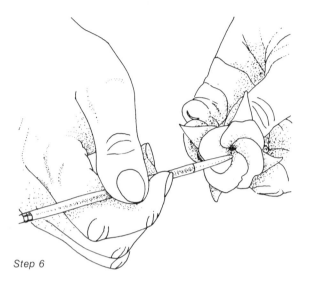

Step 6

Step 7
To wire the flower, curve an 8 cm length of cotton-covered wire at one end. Dip this hook into egg white and then push the wire through a ball of green paste the size of a small pea so that the hook is embedded in it. Hollow the top slightly and then insert the sharp end of the fuchsia flower. Support the flower with cotton wool and allow it to dry thoroughly. If necessary, touch up the flower with food colouring.

Carnation

Flower

Step 1
Roll out a small piece of paste. Cut out a circle. Using the handle of a paint brush or a rounded

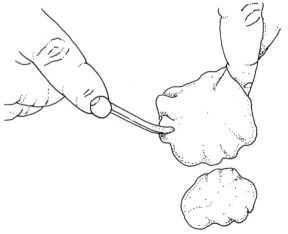

Carnation — Step 1

skewer, roll the handle all around the edge of the circle to stretch and flute it. Be careful not to tear the paste by pressing too hard. The circumference of your circle should now be double its original size and it should be quite frilly.

Step 2
Gently place this circle over a supporting circle of foil. Using your brush press the centre down to form a base and allow the outer edges to remain resting over the foil. Depending on the size of the circle you have chosen you will require three or four of these circles.

Step 3
After the second circle is fluted, paint a little egg white and gently lay your second layer over the first. Using the end of your paint brush, press together so that they join. Space the outer edges to avoid them joining and tearing.

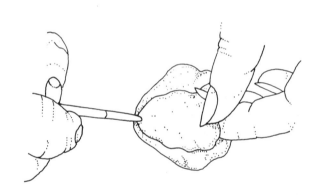

Step 3

Step 4
Repeat for the third and fourth layers. If your flower is looking very compact it may be necessary to fold the fourth circle into quarters to allow room to fit it into the centre.

Step 5
Gently ease the paste into the required shape for your flower by using the back of the paint brush. After the flower is completed remove from the foil support and pinch the back of it into a pointed shape ready to insert flower into a calyx.

Calyx

Step 1
To make a calyx (which for the carnation is heavier than usual), hollow out some paste about the size of a marble into a cup shape, thin the edges and then cut into five equal sections.

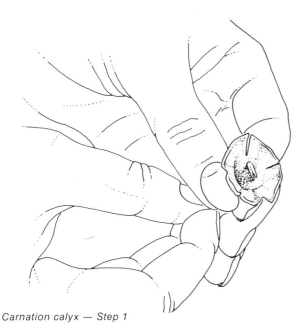

Carnation calyx — Step 1

Step 1

In brown moulding paste, make a cone shape the desired size. Attach this cone of paste to a toothpick dipped in egg white. Stick the toothpick into a block of Oasis and leave the cone to dry.

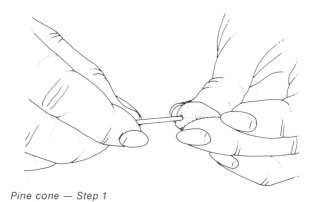

Pine cone — Step 1

Step 2

Cut each section into a pointed shape.

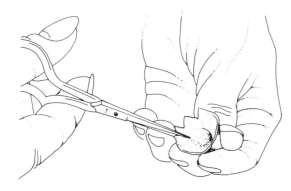

Step 2

Step 3

Thread a piece of covered wire with a closed hook at one end through the calyx and then stick a small ball of green paste on top inside the calyx to secure it.

If you wish, you can touch the edges of the petals with a paint brush dipped in food colouring, depending on the colour of your flower.

Step 4

Cut three lengths of white stamen 'stalks' and curl one end of each by scraping the blade of a pair of scissors along it. Dip the straight ends of these stamens into egg white and then insert them into the centre of the carnation.

Step 2

Roll out a small piece of paste fairly thinly and then cut from it a few long thin 'petals'.

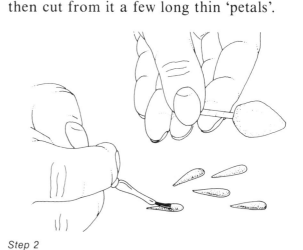

Step 2

Step 3

Start at the top by attaching three 'petals' to the point of the cone with egg white. Fold back the edge of each 'petal' very slightly.

Pine cones

Pine cones touched with gold always look rather attractive on Christmas cakes.

Step 3

Step 4
Add another row of 'petals', placing each one in the space between the two immediately above it, and again very slightly fold back each 'petal'. Continue in this way until the entire cone is covered and then allow it to dry thoroughly. Cut off the toothpick when you wish to use the cone.

Phlox

The phlox is not often described in cake decorating books, yet it is a pretty flower which is useful both for its size and the delightful effect achieved when it is wired.

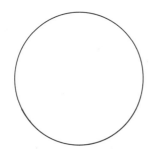

Phlox

Flower

Step 1
First make several small calyxes. Hollow out a thin cone of paste; stick a 40 mm length of thin wire with a hook at one end through the cone, and cut four thin, sharp sepals. The completed calyx is about 10 mm long. Allow to dry thoroughly.

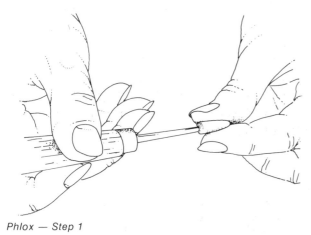

Phlox — Step 1

Step 2
Roll out some more paste fairly thinly. Cut out a circle from the template. Gently flute the edges of the circle, using your paint brush handle. From the outside of the circle, cut five equal sections to 3 mm or so from the centre. Shape each petal by cutting off its corners and then rounding off its edges.

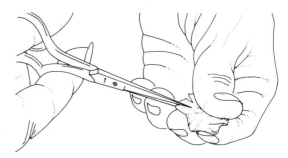

Step 2

Step 3
Form a small sharp narrow cone, about 17 mm long, from white paste. Paint egg white onto the top of the cone, and attach it to the circle, making a hole in the centre with a sharp instrument.

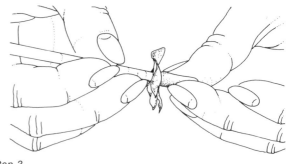

Step 3

Step 4
Paint egg white into the calyx and then insert the flower. Allow this to dry.

Bud

To make a bud, roll a small piece of paste into a ball the size of a pea and then shape it to a sharp point on one side. Mark lines on the point by using a small pair of scissors and then twist the paste slightly. Insert the bud into a calyx after touching with egg white.

Make up small groups of these flowers and buds by taping the stems together.

Phlox buds

Facing: Moulded briar roses, forget-me-nots, apple blossom, hyacinth, fuchsias, carnations and frangipani.

Centre: Moulded briar roses, sweet peas, daisies and pansies are shown here in various stages of making and colouring. Sprays of each variety show how realistically they may be presented. The colour wheel also shown here will help in mixing colours to achieve various blends and tonings.

Photo: Richard Cutler

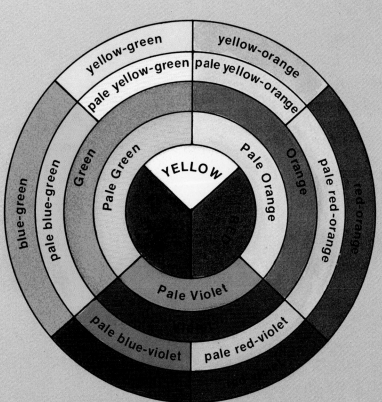

Pansy

Calyx

Step 1
Roll a ball of paste to the size of a large pea. Hollow out the ball with a modelling tool or thick knitting needle, then thin it by pressing it between your thumb and middle finger.

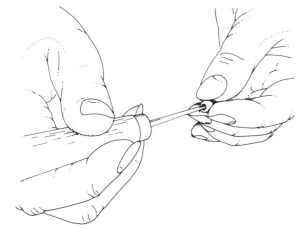

Pansy calyx — Step 1

Step 2
Cut this flat shape into five and cut each piece into a sharp petal shape.

Step 3
Dip a piece of covered wire, bent into a closed hook at one end, into egg white and slip it through the calyx you have just made. Curve the wire slightly at the calyx. Allow this to dry thoroughly. (When making pansies, it is a good idea to make the calyxes well in advance.)

Step 3

Petals

Step 1
Take another ball of gum paste and roll out thinly. Cut out two petals using pattern A, then

Facing: Moulded pansies, sweetpeas, orchids, phlox and pine cones.

mark them with veins by pressing them between your palms. Flute the round edges of each petal slightly with the handle of your paint brush, then place them aside to set.

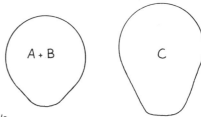

Pansy petals

Step 2
Stick these petals (which should still be pliable) into the calyx with egg white, the left one slightly overlapping the right one. These are the top two petals of the pansy.

Step 3
Cut two petals using pattern B. Press each one between your hands to mark it and then flute each one slightly along the rounded edge. Put them aside to set a little. Attach these two petals to the calyx, just over the lower edges of the first two.

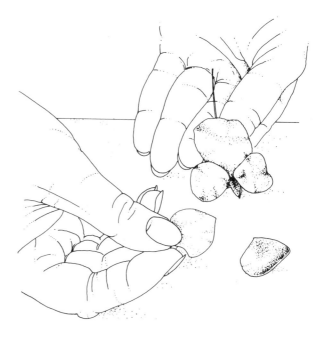

Assembling the pansy

Step 4
Cut one petal of pattern C, flute the lower edge gently, then put it aside to set. Finally, attach this to the calyx with egg white, either just overlapping or just touching the last two petals.

When all the petals have dried you may then paint your flower. For instructions on colouring and painting see page 125.

With white royal icing in a small writing tube, pipe a small crescent shape on the lower edge of the centre opening and then an inverted 'V' shape at the top of the opening. When this icing is dry, paint the crescent shape deep yellow.

Leaves

Pansy leaves are just as pretty as the flowers. You will have to make them smaller than they are naturally, but it is a good idea to look at some real ones for accuracy. (See sample facing page 63.)

Sweet Pea

The sweet pea often seems to be overlooked in cake decorating. Yet its wide range of colours and suitability for wiring makes it an ideal choice. The flower has two bud stages and a full blown flower, all of which are needed to make up a spray. Tendrils may be included if required. If cutters are used for petals, cut away the point before use.

Bud 1

Step 1
Take a small piece of gum paste and attach this to a hooked piece of cotton-covered wire so that a long bullet shape is formed. This centre is best allowed to dry overnight before continuing. Since it best to have a variety of sizes of flower, make the bullets in a wide range of sizes. With practice you will know how large or small you prefer your flower to be.

Step 2
Either using cutters or freehand, make a small petal; paint a little water or egg white all around the edges and fold this around the centre so it is completely enclosed. Trim around the joins if necessary. Set this bud aside to dry.

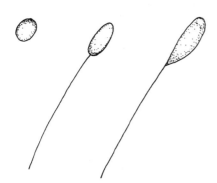

Sweet pea bud — Stage 1

Bud 2

Step 3
Take a bud that has been completed to the stage described above. Again either freehand or using a medium-sized cutter, make a petal that is larger than the previous one. Flute the outer edges by stretching the outer part with the paint brush handle. Be careful not to make indentations on the inside of the petal while doing this. With water or egg white, paint an arrow shape down the centre of the petal with the two points towards yourself.

Step 4
Lay the bud over the petal so that it stands upright. With a little pressure, attach the centre and lower base to the petal. Pinch the lower edge of the petal at the point where the wire is attached to ensure it is held firmly together. Set this bud aside to dry.

Sweet pea bud — Stage 2

Full blown flower

Step 5
Take a bud that has been completed to Bud 2 stage. This time make a large petal; flute and stretch this in the same way as the previous petal. Paint another arrow of water or egg white down the centre of the petal. This time, however, do not extend it the full length of the petal because the top part does not need to be attached.

Step 6
Lay the bud over the petal, press along the wet area and pinch at the base. Bend the petal back away from the flower so that it stands out more than the previous petal. Insert the wire into a piece of Oasis and allow to dry.

A five sepal calyx may be attached if required. Tendrils may be made by twisting suitably coloured cotton-covered wire around a fine skewer then removing the skewer from the centre. These may be stretched and twisted to

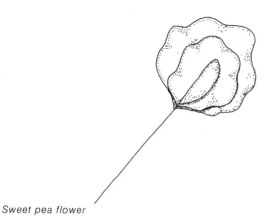
Sweet pea flower

the desired shape. The sweet pea looks effective if the outside edges are coloured in a darker shade (see page 125 for colouring).

Cattleya orchid

Centre

Method 1

Step 1
Roll some white paste the size of a large pea into a cylindrical shape about 25 mm long, tapering at either end to a slight point. The underside of the cylinder should be slightly flat and the top slightly rounded.

Step 2
Make two small 'eyes' in one end using a pin or other sharp object. Set this centre aside to dry a little.

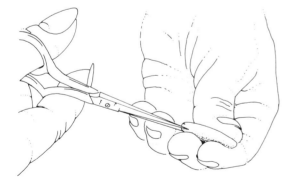
Cattleya centre — Method 1

Step 3
If you wish to wire the orchid, insert the wire into this centre which must dry thoroughly before the assembly.

Method 2

Step 1
Make a very thin roll of white paste about 25 mm long. Make two cuts in one end with

your small scissors and then flatten these three parts.

Step 2
Curve the centre piece downward and the two side ones slightly inward. Set aside to dry.

Step 3
When wiring the flower, insert the wire through this centre and leave the flower to dry thoroughly.

Trumpet

Step 1
Take a piece of paste about the size of a small apple. Break off a small piece and roll it out so that one side is slightly thicker than the other.

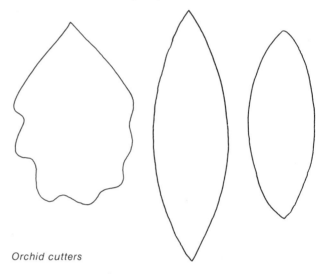
Orchid cutters

Place the orchid trumpet cutter or template so that the curved part is on the thicker part of the paste.

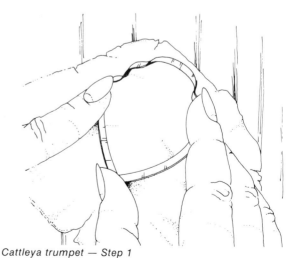
Cattleya trumpet — Step 1

Step 2
Cut out the trumpet. Fold it in half from the point to the centre of the curve so that the upper surface remains outside.

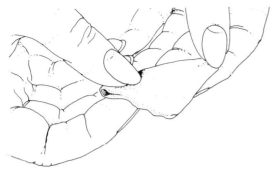

Step 2

Step 3
Using your paint brush, your hand or a skewer, flute or frill the edge of the round section. This edge should be as frilly as possible.

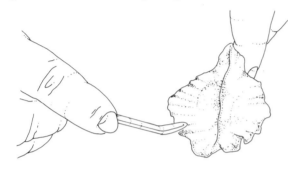

Step 3

Step 4
Paint a little egg white onto the inside of the pointed end of the trumpet. At this point, put

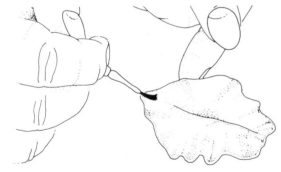

Step 4 (i)

the centre you have made onto the trumpet, wrapping the latter around the centre. Slightly fold back each side of the curve to open the trumpet but do not make it too flat or too wide

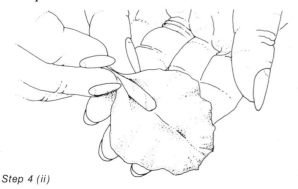

Step 4 (ii)

open. Cut off the excess at an upward angle at the sharp end of the trumpet.

Step 5
Place the trumpet on a piece of foam rubber and allow it to dry, propping it up gently with some cotton wool if necessary, to keep its shape.

Step 5

Make one or two more of these trumpets.

To complete

Step 1
Break off another portion of paste and roll it out fairly thinly. Cut three long cattleya orchid petals and, with your scalpel blade, mark lines along the length of the petal. Let the petals set on the cardboard roll.

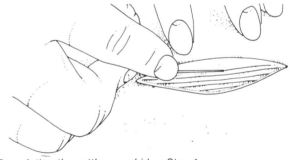

Completing the cattleya orchid — Step 1

Step 2
Roll out some more paste and cut two wider cattleya orchid petals. Fold the petals in half with the mark of the fold uppermost. Flute the edges of the petal but leave its base (the less pointed end) plain. Do the same with the second petal, then let the two set on the cardboard roll.

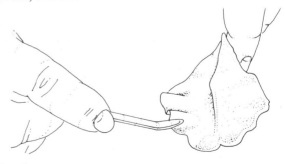

Step 2

Step 3

Roll some paste into a ball about the size of a large pea and press it onto a foil-lined shallow patty tin. If this is too deep, shape a piece of foil to the required size.

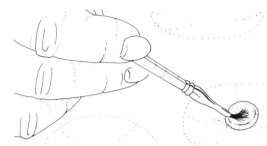

Step 3

Step 4

Paint egg white onto the flattened ball of paste. Take one long petal and stick it in the paste pointing away from you. Then attach the other two long petals as shown.

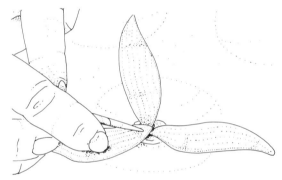

Step 4

Step 5

Paint some more egg white onto the centre of these petals, then add the two wider petals as shown.

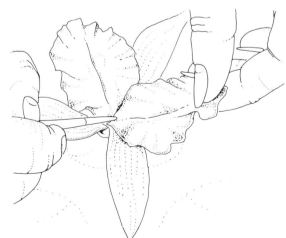

Step 5

Step 6

Press the narrow end of the dry trumpet into the centre of these petals holding the front part quite high up.

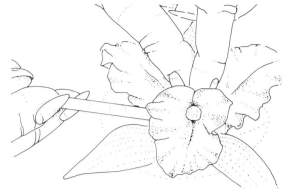

Step 6

Step 7

Place small pieces of cotton wool under each of the long petals to shape them as desired.

Set the flower aside to dry.

Make up more orchids in the same way.

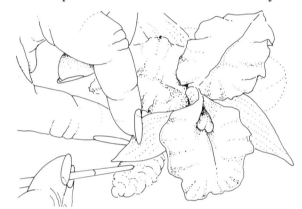

Step 7

Cymbidium orchids

Trumpet and tongue

Step 1

Roll a small piece of white paste twice the size of a large pea into a cylinder about 15 mm long with rounded ends. Using your paint brush handle, press a hollow into its length and then curve the cylinder slightly. Make several of these and allow to dry.

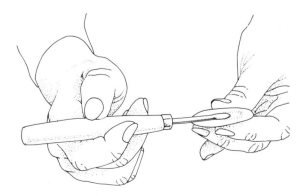

Cymbidium tongue

Step 2
Take some paste (about the size of a small apple). Roll out a piece and cut a cymbidium trumpet similar to that for the cattleya orchid. Make two nicks each about 2 mm deep into the petal at either end of the three scallops.

Step 3
Flute the three scallops as much as possible, curving the unworked edges upwards and gently coaxing the front curved part downwards. Let the trumpet dry on the foam rubber or a cardboard roll so that the scalloped part hangs over its edge.

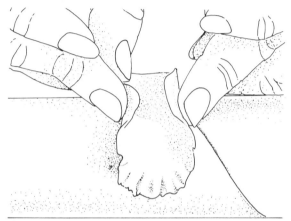

Cymbidium trumpet

Step 4
Take a small piece of paste. Roll two cylinders about 2 mm thick and 10 mm long, each one tapering to nothing. Paint a little egg white onto the back of each and stick them to the orchid trumpet from the centre of the throat forwards. If necessary, prop the trumpet with cotton wool until set and dry.

Make several more trumpets in this way and set them aside to dry.

To Complete

Step 1
Roll out some paste and cut two pairs of side cymbidium orchid petals. When making pairs, remember that you will need a left and a right

Step 1 (i)

petal for each pair, so you must reverse the cutters or template. Using your scalpel blade, mark lines close together on each petal from tip to tip. Flute the edges of each petal slightly. Place both pairs face up over the cardboard roll.

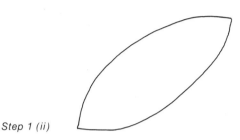

Step 1 (ii)

Step 2
Cut the fifth petal and mark it also with close lines from tip to tip, flute it and set it over the cardboard roll.

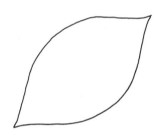

Step 2

Step 3
Roll some paste into a ball about the size of a large pea. Press this ball into the centre of a foil-lined patty tin.

Step 4
Paint egg white onto the flattened ball of paste. Add the single centre top petal. Take the two pairs of side petals and stick them to this piece of paste, using the end of your paint brush to press them gently into the paste if necessary.

Step 5
Add the trumpet (it must be thoroughly dry) and press it firmly into the centre. Raise the trumpet to the correct position.

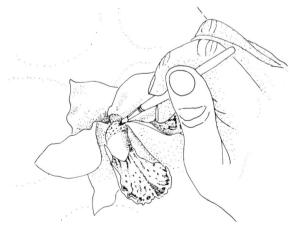

Completing the cymbidium orchid

Step 6

Add the centre or tongue of the orchid, made previously, to the centre of the flower, curving the tongue forward.

No calyx is needed for either of the orchids.

Leaves

These are usually quite long and slender. One of the side petal cutters can be used to make a suitable size leaf. Vein as required.

Bud

Orchid buds look rather clumsy so it is better to make a spray of flowers in graded sizes rather than buds.

Phalaenopsis orchid

The phalaenopsis orchid is another popular orchid, otherwise known as the moth orchid. The cake between pages 94-95 has a beautiful display of these. Note that the flowers have been made in a variety of sizes to suit the size of each cake. Since this flower has a large number of pieces to be made, you may like to have a real orchid available to study features such as size, shape and colour.

Flower

Step 1

This orchid is quite a flat flower, so you will not need to curve the pieces very much. Roll out some gum paste and, using the following pattern, cut out three of the narrower petals. Finger these smooth and fine them down. Mark out veins and then set them into a shallow patty tin to give them only a soft curve or, if you prefer, support them with pieces of foil which allow them to dry in the desired shape.

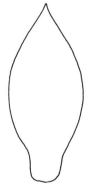

Phalaenopsis orchid — Step 1

Step 2

Roll out more gum paste. This time cut out two of the larger rounded petals. Note that these have more pronounced markings and veins. See the flowers between pages 94-95. Place these in a patty tin or over foil to allow for a soft curve while they are drying.

Step 2

Step 3

Now using either the pattern given or your blossom petal cutter, cut out two side lobes. If the cutter is being used, cut off the points from the base ends. Gently finger these and push your thumb into the centre while holding each one in the palm of your hand, or else place them on a piece of foam and press gently so that a soft rounded cup-like effect is achieved.

Step 3

Step 4

Roll out more gum paste, this time slightly thicker than that used for the petals. Either using the pattern given or freehand, cut out one or two throat pieces (allow one spare throat for breakages). This throat, or trumpet, is a little unusual because it has long tendril-like sections that curve back into the flower.

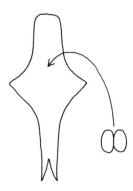

Step 4

Step 5

Take two medium-length stamen cottons. Curve them with the fingers and then insert one into each of the points at the 'Vee' part of the throat. Do this for both of the throats being made. Pinch slightly at each point to attach securely.

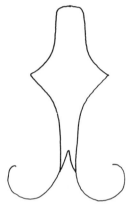

Step 5

Step 6

Using your piece of foam, place the throat on it and then gently press down in the centre. Run your finger along the inside, so that the throat curves up and around at the sides. This may be done in the palm of the hand if you prefer.

Step 6

Step 7

Take a small piece of gum paste the size of a pea. Shape it to an oval, and then, using the back of a scalpel blade, push down in the middle to divide it into two equal sections that are still attached together and are also still smooth on the underside. Allow to dry. This is then placed slightly above the centre of the throat. Attach it with royal icing.

Step 8

The column to this flower is quite small. It is in the shape of a "C" and scooped out in the centre. This is easier to make by moulding it freehand. Allow the base to be flatter at the end.

After you have made all the pieces required for these orchids, allow them to dry.

How to assemble

Step 1

Take a large square of foil and some very stiff royal icing. Shape the foil to a very gentle curve, then make up a piping bag. Using your star tube, pipe a medium size star in the centre of the foil.

Assemble the three narrower petals so that one is at the top and the other two are placed to the left and right of this and down low enough to enable you to fit your other pieces in place. See illustration.

How to assemble

Step 2

Set the two larger petals to the left and right of the top petal. Ensure that they are held in place securely and place a little more royal icing if it is needed.

Step 3

Next, take your throat piece, being gentle so as not to damage it. Lay this between the two lower narrower petals so that the base fits in securely in the lower centre. Be careful not to disturb the stamen cottons and the centre piece you have already inserted.

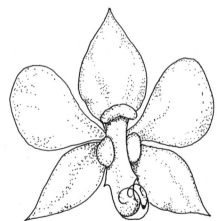

Step 3

Facing: This sulphur-crested cockatoo by Mrs Cathleen Bowen is made of cake. The feathers were made individually and wired on. Of particular note are the finely detailed gum leaves the bird is holding in its claw.

The strong colours of tropical flowers have been cleverly handled by Mrs Mary Lynas in this lovely arrangement of hibiscus, frangipani, ginger lily and dendrobium orchids set against the background of a raffia fan.

Made by Mrs Noelle Barnard, this cake shows plenty of skill. It has beautiful two-tone pink lace and all the features often requested for a wedding cake.

Step 4
Place the column piece above the throat with the curve towards you. A pair of tweezers will be required for this. This piece forms a curve with the curve of the throat and stamen cottons.

Step 5
Finally attach the two lobe pieces at the top left and right sides of the throat. Gently curve them in towards the centre of the flower. Ensure that they are placed just a little under the throat. If more royal icing is required, pipe a little more where it is needed; but do not be too generous with the icing, otherwise the flower will look heavy and untidy.

Support any parts of the flower which will not remain in place with either foil or cotton wool. Be careful not to damage pieces when this is removed.

No leaves are required.

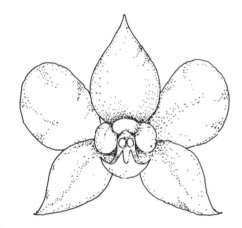

Step 7

Calyx

A calyx may be added after the flower is completely dry. Do not attempt this if you are a beginner, or the result may be a broken flower.

The flower should be laid upside down on a thick layer of cotton wool. A calyx can be made in the same way as the bluebell is made (see page 72). Attach a piece of cotton covered wire, moisten the inside of the calyx and then gently lay this on the back of the flower and press into place. Allow to dry before wiring flowers together.

See page 125 for colouring instructions.

Facing: Mrs Margaret McGann has used peace roses in the arrangement on this cake. Hyacinths and lily-of-the valley complete the arrangement.

Forget-me-nots

Flower

Step 1
Take a ball of gum paste and roll it out very thinly.

Step 2
Take a forget-me-not cutter and cut a flower from the paste.

Step 3
Hold the cutter on a piece of foam rubber, insert the rounded end of a hair curler pin into the cutter and gently ease the paste off the cutter, at the same time pressing it gently into the foam. This gives the flower a small cup shape. Do not press too hard otherwise the paste will tear away.

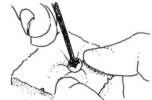

Step 3 — Forget-me-not

Step 4
Push a stamen through the centre of the flower while the latter is still wet. Touch a little egg white into the centre of the flowers before inserting the stamen, or else first dip the head of the stamen in egg white or royal icing to secure it. Doing the flowers in this way allows you to wire them together in small sprays.

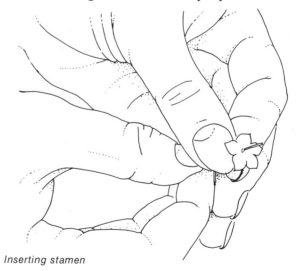

Inserting stamen

Buds

These are made by rubbing a small piece of paste onto the end of a stamen. Leave the end slightly rounded.

Lily of the valley

This flower is very similar to the forget-me-not but it does not have any petals.

Flower

Step 1
Take a small piece of gum paste about the size of a small pea.

Step 2
Using the handle of your paint brush, insert this into the paste to hollow it out to form a small cup shape.

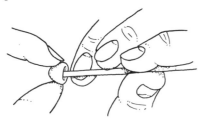

Lily of the Valley — Step 2

Step 3
Insert one long stamen into the centre and pull it through. Allow the tip of the stamen to just show through at the base of the flower.

Step 3

Buds

These are made simply by rolling a small piece of paste onto the end of a stamen. Shape to a small point.

Lilies of the valley are illustrated facing page 31.

Bluebell/hyacinth

Flower

Step 1
Take a ball of gum paste. Break off a piece about the size of a large pea and roll it into a ball. Push a rounded skewer into the paste and, gently turning the paste, hollow it out to a cone shape.

Step 2
When the paste has been sufficiently hollowed out, you will be able to thin the outer edge of the 'bell' shape with the tips of thumb and

Bluebell/hyacinth — Step 1

forefinger. Press this outer edge until it is quite thin and then smooth the inside of this shape again with your skewer.

Step 2

Step 3
Take your small scissors and make a cut straight towards the centre from the outer edge. Turn the 'bell' and make another cut opposite the first, but slightly off the halfway mark. Make a cut between these first two cuts and then two further cuts on the other side of the 'bell' so that you have five square petals. Cut from the centre of the outer edge of each petal curving slightly towards the base. Complete the other side of the petal in the same way and then repeat the procedure with the other four petals. Press each petal between your thumb and middle finger to thin it and then pinch its point. Curve the petals slightly backwards.

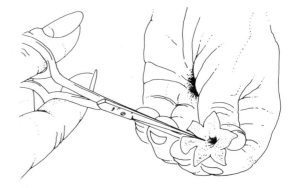

Step 3

Step 4
Touch some egg white into the centre of the flower. Take three yellow stamens each about 30 mm long and insert them into the centre of the flower so that the heads of the stamens just show above the flower's opening. Leave the long ends of the stamens showing through the base as these will be used to wire the flowers to a single stem when they are thoroughly dry.

Make a number of these and set them aside to dry.

Hyacinth

Proceed exactly the same way for the hyacinth as for the bluebell but insert a single 30 mm stamen, drawing it right through so that the stamen head rests in the base of the flower. The hyacinth has six petals instead of five.

Wiring bluebells and hyacinths

Take a thin piece of cotton-covered wire about 250 mm long. Cut a length of tape to approximately the same length and cut it lengthways into three. Take one of the smaller bluebells or hyacinths by the stamens protruding from the base, in such a way that the flower is at the end of the wire and parallel to it. Turn the wire and stamen into the tape with the right hand, stretching the tape as you go.

Continue taping for another 10-15 mm before adding the next flower. Proceed in this way until your stem of flowers is about 60 mm long.

Make up a number of stems of flowers like this and set them aside until required.

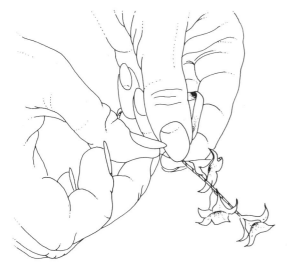

Wiring bluebells and hyacinths

Buds

These are made in the same way as for the forget-me-not. Use cotton-covered wire instead of a stamen and make them large enough to be appropriate for their flower.

See cakes facing pages 39 and 70 for pictures of these fowers.

Azalea

Azaleas are a versatile flower because they come in so many shades and sizes. They can be very open single flowers or dense, full blooms with many petals. The azaleas seen on the christening cake facing page 31 have been made by using the frangipani cutter. They may also be made either freehand or with a briar rose cutter. (See page 47 for templates of these.)

Flower

Step 1
Take a ball of gum paste, roll it out thinly and then cut out five petals. Flute each petal gently on the outer edges, then lay them over the handle of a wooden spoon to allow them to take up a curved shape. Allow the petals to dry.

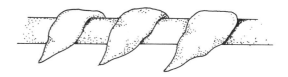

Azalea — Step 1

Step 2
Make a cone shape from foil. Take a petal and, using a little royal icing, pipe a small amount of icing at the base. Lay the next petal so that it overlaps the first one by 5 mm on the right-hand side.

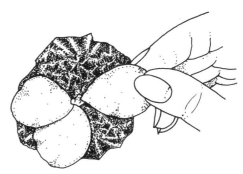

Step 2

Step 3
Continue in this way and for the last petal, pipe some icing on the underside of the first petal and

tuck the last one underneath the first. Allow the icing to set before removing the flower from the foil. If you prefer to attach your petals together while they are still soft, paint a little water or egg white onto the lower right-hand edge of each petal and overlap in the same way. Make sure that the point of the flower is rounded off to a smooth closed point by pressing the flower gently at its base.

Alternative flower

Some azaleas have a definite crease along the centre of each petal. Some also appear to have one petal which does not follow in the usual pattern. To produce an azalea with a crease line, follow the method as already described but after fluting the outer edges of each petal, fold the petal in half along its length and then open it out again. Do not press too hard otherwise your petals will crack. The wider part of the petal may be pinched a little so as to hold the fold line. Ensure that the fold lines are to the outside of the flower when you assemble them together.

Assemble these flowers using a cone shaped piece of foil for support, but place the last petal so that it sits on top of the first petal instead of tucking it underneath. Pipe a small amount of icing at the base of the flower and insert eight fine-tipped stamens plus one longer one to represent the stigma. Stamens are usually the same length as the petals, with the stigma protruding a further 5-10 mm. If you are making very small azaleas or the large full flowers it is a good idea to take some real flowers and pull them apart to see how many petals they have. This is also helpful to achieve realistic colours and you can make templates from the real petals.

Buds

These are made by taking a piece of gum paste and moulding it to a bullet shape. Point one end slightly. Pinch a few lines, or mark them in with a skewer to give the impression of petals. Most of your buds will need to be wired, but some can be left without wire to be inserted into spaces in your arrangement.

Azalea buds

Calyx

The calyx of the azalea is very small, so you may wish to wire both the flowers and buds and then paint a small calyx after they are dry. Otherwise a calyx may be made from a small piece of gum paste. Using the end of your paint brush, insert the handle into the paste and hollow out to a small cone. Cut five slits into this and gently pinch each section to a small point. Insert a hooked piece of cotton-covered wire into this calyx, moisten the inside with a little water or egg white and then place the completed flower or bud into it. Support both the flower and calyx while you allow it to dry or, if the flower is dry, turn it upside down until the calyx is dry.

Leaves

Azalea leaves are softer than many others. They are oval in shape and slightly hairy. Leaves may be cut out freehand, veined and then either wired or left separate to fill empty spaces in your spray. If you intend to wire the leaves it is best to attach stamen cottons to them instead of wire. These are then taped together into a circular spray with buds and flowers in the centre. Naturally it may not always be possible to present these flowers in this way but it does look very attractive if your leaves are fine and small.

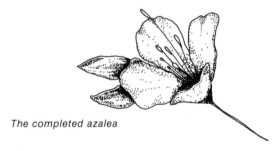

The completed azalea

Daffodil

Daffodils are glorious flowers for use on cakes. They are particularly suitable on spring wedding cakes. Flowers may be coloured in shades of lemon, yellow, gold, white and even a soft apricot pink so they are adaptable for any occasion needing lemon as its central colour scheme. Jonquils are really only a smaller version of this flower.

Daffodils may be made progressively in three stages, allowed to dry and then assembled or, if you feel confident, they can be assembled progressively after the centre cone or trumpet has dried. If real flowers are available while you are making these it is a good idea to keep one on hand for reference.

Flower

Step 1

Take enough paste for the size of flower you wish to make. Shape this piece of paste to a tear drop. Using your rounded skewer, hollow this out so that you have a fine trumpet shape. The base will be narrower than the top; it will also be smooth and rounded to allow for easy assembly of the flower.

Daffodil — Step 1

Step 2

The top of the trumpet can be ruffled and fluted by stretching the outer edges with your brush handle. This fluted area can be left standing upright or curved out and under slightly. If you are making a jonquil, the trumpet is not very deep and it is usually a cup shape rather than frilled. Daffodils can also have a tailored looking trumpet. This is achieved by making small cut edges at the top and turning them back instead of stretching.

Step 2

Step 3

Take a piece of hooked cotton-covered wire, moisten and insert it into the base, and smooth the paste at the point where it is attached.

Step 4

Place six fine-tipped stamens into the trumpet. If they will not remain in place use a little royal icing. Allow the trumpet to dry by resting it gently upside-down on a bed of cotton wool.

Step 4

Step 5

Take another piece of paste about the same size as the first. Form into a tear drop shape. Insert your rounded skewer into the paste and hollow out until you have made a fine cone shape. If you find this part difficult you may cut out the appropriate size circle instead.

Step 6

Make three slits a little deeper than halfway into your cone. Cut off excess paste and shape a pointed end which has a soft curve closer to the base. Your twisted petals thus have a curved side-edge, with a shallow point at the top. Do this for each of the three petals. If you are using the circle method divide it into three and, using your scalpel, cut each petal as already described. Form a cup shape at the base, moisten the inside and attach this first layer of petals to the trumpet. Naturally the wire from the trumpet will have to be pushed through the base of the layer of petals.

Step 6

Step 7

Make a second layer of three petals in the same way as described above. Moisten and attach so that the next three petals fit into the spaces between the others. Firm and cup the base of the flower and allow to dry on a piece of Oasis. If your flower needs support, use a piece of foil shaped into the required form. Do not forget to space your petals evenly with the back of your brush and bend the petals back slightly where needed. The two layers of petals may be dried first on foil before they are attached. If you prefer to assemble your flowers when they are dry use egg white or a little royal icing for assembly. The six outer petals may be cut out individually and attached separately around the cone, if you cannot master the previous method.

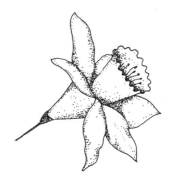

Step 7

Buds

Daffodil buds are not very attractive as they look too heavy, so it is best not to use them.

Leaves

Daffodil leaves are not very suitable for use on cakes. I prefer to use leaves from another flower in the arrangement.

Calyx

Rather than make a calyx, when taping your flowers with florist's tape pull some up over the lower part of the flower to give the impression of a calyx.

Gypsophila (Baby tears)

One of my own favourite flowers, gypsophila is often used for weddings and incorporated into table arrangements. There are two varieties, the larger single flower and the smaller tight compact variety. Since these flowers are so small I will only give directions for the compact flowers.

Flower

Step 1
Attach a very small ball of paste either to a fine piece of cotton-covered wire or, if you intend to use these flowers in clusters, to the cotton from a stamen. These latter will then be wired into a spray by attaching them to a piece of wire with florist's tape.

Ease the paste a little way down the piece of wire. Take your fine skewer or hat pin and insert it into the paste to form seven small holes around the outer edge of the ball of paste and make a hole into the centre.

Gypsophila — Step 1

Step 2
Using a flat-ended pair of tweezers gently pinch seven 'petals' around the outside of this paste so that each hole forms the curve of the petal. Pinch into the centre of the flower as well so that the centre hole is raised slightly.

Step 2

Step 3
Taking the skewer again, adjust each petal by pushing the petals out in the centre and ensure

that the centre of the flower is slightly closed. If you prefer to have your flowers open, use the blunt end of your skewer to press a small flat centre in the flower. These flowers are all white but have a pale green centre when fully opened.

Step 3

Jasmine

Jasmine is another useful flower for arrangements on wedding cakes. There are two different types pictured facing page 55 and page 95. The flowers used facing page 55 give a lovely airy touch to the table centrepiece. They are very fragile but worth perservering with because they look so realistic. The jasmine used on the wedding cake facing page 95 is smaller and is a more useful type for weddings that require a touch of pink. Try making both varieties before choosing which you prefer.

Flower

Step 1
Take a small ball of gum-paste the size of a small pea. Using the handle of your paint brush, insert it into the centre of the paste and hollow out the ball to a fine bell shape. Do this by continually pressing the handle against the paste, at the same time rotating the paste in your hand so that all areas are thinned out.

Step 2
Make five evenly-spaced cuts into the bell shape. Make your cuts deeper down almost to the centre of the flower for the longer petalled variety. The shorter petalled flowers have a shorter cut which does not go as deeply into the centre.

Step 3
Cut the sharp corners off each petal. Press the petals between your fingers to neaten the curved edges.

Step 4
Twist your petals backwards and curve them slightly at various angles. Study some real jasmine growing as the best model to follow for twisting and bending these petals.

Step 5
Insert thin cotton-covered wire into the base of the flower, and then gently ease some of the paste down part of the wire to elongate the flower. You may do this by rolling the wire backwards and forwards between your fingers, at the same time easing the paste against the wire.

Step 6
Place one stamen only in the centre of the flower, letting it just show above the centre. The stamens should be white, lemon or very pale green.

Buds

There are usually many more buds than flowers on a spray of jasmine. Take a thin piece of cotton-covered wire, hook one end and moisten with a little water. Using a very small piece of paste, roll both the wire and paste between your fingers so that the wire is encased by the paste at the hooked end. Some of your buds can be quite long. Allow approximately 5 mm of paste along the wire. Squeeze the top gently to achieve a slightly rounded top. Bend these buds and twist as required. Again, study some real flowers to help achieve a realistic appearance.

Calyx

Jasmine has such a minute calyx that it would be impractical to make it separately. Paint it on after the flower dries. It is brownish-green in colour.

Leaves

Jasmine leaves are quite attractive although they are not often used. Each leaf is made up of a cluster of nine small leaves which grow along the stems in pairs. Use a real leaf to cut out your template pattern. Attach a stamen cotton to each of these instead of using wire. Tape them together onto a piece of wire with florist's tape.

Jasmine

Freesia

Freesia is an unusual choice of flower for the wedding cake facing page 94. The freesia is quite a long tubular flower; it comes in many different colours.

Flower

Step 1
Take a piece of gum paste 2-3 cm long and shape to a tear drop. Hollow it out by pressing the rounded skewer into the paste. Keep rotating the paste in your hand and press continually on the outer edges; this will give you a fine bell shape.

Step 2
Cut each petal by making six slits 10 mm long into the bell shape, then shape each petal into a curve which is slightly pointed. This point can be pinched by pressing the petal at its centre between your thumb and forefinger.

Step 3
Arrange the petals so that every alternate one curves out slightly more than the others. Make sure that the flower tapers to be thinner at its base. Leave to dry in an upturned egg carton. If you need to attach a piece of wire, do this before the flower dries. Insert a hooked piece of wire at the base, and pinch the paste into the wire so that the flower or bud will be firmly attached.

Bud

Take a piece of gum paste according to the size of bud you wish to make. Note that the buds on the cake pictures go from a small 5 mm in length through to the same length as the full flowers.

Step 1
If your buds are to be small, shape them into a small tubular shape slightly pointed at the tip. The larger buds are wider and longer although they taper to a smaller thickness at the base.

Step 2
Some other buds may be made by taking a piece of gum paste 2-3 cm in length. Hollow out into a tube by inserting your rounded skewer deep into the paste, as for the flower.

Step 3
Cut six slits no deeper than 10 mm into the paste. Then cut each petal to a curved shape, almost pointed in the centre.

Step 4
Smooth out each petal with your fingers, then gently overlap them and close the flower. Do not press too hard otherwise some of your petals may fall off. Leave only a slight opening.

Calyx

The calyx of the freesia is quite small. It may be attached to the flower while it is dry or soft or, if you prefer, it may just be painted on. Make the calyx in the same way as for the azalea on page 74.

Flowers and buds are attached in long sprays using two or three buds, a closed flower and two or three open flowers. For example, look at the arrangement on the top tier of the cake facing page 94. Allow for extra length in your wire to achieve this effect. Look at a spray of real flowers if possible, to give a realistic effect to your sprays.

Freesia

Leaves

These are slender and long so it is best to use leaves from another flower in your arrangement, or ivy leaves.

Primula

Primulas are illustrated on a cake between pages 30-31. They come in shades of pink, mauve and white. It is another of the small dainty flowers suitable for many occasions. These flowers may be made freehand or you may use a cutter or template.

Primula cutters

Flower

Step 1
Take a piece of paste the size of a pea. Using the handle of your paint brush, hollow out the piece to form a small cone.

Step 2
Using your fine scissors, make five deep cuts into the cone to form five evenly-spaced petals.

Step 3
Cut out a small vee from the top of each petal centre but do not make these too deep.

Step 4
Cut away the sharp points from the outer edges of the petals to form a soft curve. This will give a heart-shaped effect to each of your petals.

Step 5
Smooth and fine down your petals by pressing each one between the fingers; bend each one back a little to give the flower an open look.

Step 6
Attach a piece of fine cotton-covered wire to the flower by making a small hook at one end and pushing it through the centre of the flower.

Primula — Step 6

Step 7
Twist and pinch the base of the flower close to the wire so that it is securely attached at the base. A small yellow dot may be painted in the centre to finish off the flower. The flowers on the cake pictured have had a small green centre added together with a few very short green stamen cottons which complement the colour scheme used on the cake.

You may prefer to make your flower in one piece by using the cutter or template shown. Roll out a piece of paste and cut out the flower. Place the shape on a piece of foam and press the center with the rounded end of a hair curler pin. Attach a piece of cotton-covered wire by inserting it through the centre of the flower.

Bud

Primula buds are made by rubbing a very small piece of paste on to the end of a stamen. Shape to a small point.

Calyx

Primula flowers and buds are too small for a separate calyx, so it is best to paint one on after the flowers and buds are completely dry.

Primulas usually come on medium stems with many flowers in a circular cluster down the length of the stem. It is, however, more practical to arrange them in small clusters of two buds and three or four flowers.

Leaves

These are dainty and almost heart-shaped. They may be used separately or attached to a small cluster of flowers. Cut out a leaf to the required shape and size with a scalpel, mark in veins and attach a stamen wire. Lay these leaves over a pencil or handle to give a curved shape while they dry.

The completed primula

Boronia

Boronia is a very distinctive Australian flower. There are many different colours in the boronia family and they are very popular because of their beautiful fragrance. It is a good idea to find samples of real flowers when they are in bloom so that you can copy them accurately. You may be surprised at how many varieties there are to choose from.

Brown boronia

Because of its dark colour this variety makes a good contrast. (See cake facing page 54.)

Step 1
Take a piece of paste the size of a large pea. Attach this to a hooked piece of cotton-covered wire by moistening the end of the wire and inserting it into the paste.

Step 2
Ease paste down along part of the wire by rubbing the wire and paste backwards and forwards between the thumb and forefinger. This will give a little more length to the flower.

Brown boronia — Steps 1 and 2

Step 3
Flatten the top part of the paste against your hand. Insert the rounded skewer into the paste while moving it, to allow a small fine cup to be formed.

Step 3

Step 4
Using your fine scissors, make four small cuts into this cup. Cut off excess points from each petal so that you have four small rounded petals. These petals can be left slightly closed and pushed forward into the flower centre or left open. They do not usually open up very far.

Step 5
Either push a very short stamen deep into the centre or push your wire back into the flower a little to achieve the same effect.

Step 5

Bud

Use a small rounded ball of paste. Attach in the same way as for the flower.

Calyx

The boronia calyx is very small so it is easier, and a softer effect is achieved, if a calyx is painted on after the flower is dry.

Leaves

Boronia leaves are very small so usually only the flowers are presented on a cake. If you want to make leaves, use your scalpel to cut out several very small oval-shaped leaves. Attach each of these to a stamen cotton using a little water or egg white. Allow to dry then tape together onto a piece of wire with florist's tape. Assemble with the flowers.

White boronia

This variety is often used in arrangements and is particularly suitable for christenings or birthdays. (See cake between pages 30-31.)

Step 1
Take a small piece of paste the size of a small pea. Using your paint brush handle, hollow out the paste to a small cone.

Step 2
Make four cuts deep into the cone so that you have four equal-size petals.

Step 3
Cut off excess paste and cut each petal to a soft, curved point.

Step 4
Pinch each petal to a fine smooth end which is slightly rounded. Take a piece of fine cotton-covered wire. Make a small hook at one end, moisten it with water and push the other end through the flower until the hooked end is only just visible in the central base of the flower.

Step 5
Pinch the base of the flower to ensure the paste is well attached to the wire.

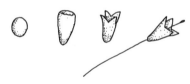

White boronia

Bud

Buds of white boronia are the same as those of the brown variety. Make buds and flowers in graded sizes so that a realistic effect is achieved when you assemble your spray. Darker lines may be painted on the buds to give an impression of petals.

Calyx

Again, these flowers are too small to make a separate calyx. Using your fine paint brush, paint a calyx onto your flowers and buds after they are completely dry.

Leaves

For this variety of boronia, leaves are slender and long. They may be made cut out freehand and attached to a stamen cotton. Mark a centre vein with the back edge of your scalpel blade.

White boronia leaves

Pink boronia

Pink boronia is also very popular for cake decoration. The only difference between pink and white boronia (apart from the colour) is that the pink has a slightly longer leaf which is rounded at the tip rather than pointed.

Daisy

The daisy is a very versatile flower when used in cake decorating. Depending on size, shape, colour and number of petals, the basic daisy flower can be adapted to form Cineraria, Flannel flowers and Everlastings, as well as the ordinary daisy varieties.

There are several methods which can be used to make daisies.

Small Easter daisy or English daisy

Step 1
Take a piece of paste the size of a large pea. Using the rounded end of your skewer, hollow out the paste to form a fine cone shape.

Step 2
Attach a piece of fine cotton-covered wire by making a small hook at one end. Moisten to attach to the paste. Push the other end into the centre of the cone and pull it down through the cone until the hooked end is only just visible through the centre. Press and pinch the paste against the outer edge of the wire to attach it firmly.

Step 3
Using your fine-pointed scissors in the right hand, and rotating the cone with your left hand, make your petals by making deep cuts into the cone. You need to leave enough space in the centre of the flower to pipe a cluster of dots with royal icing. Petals look more effective if they are only one or two centimetres wide. You may find that petals are a little wider at the outer edge than they are in the centre. If the odd petal falls off, it does not matter too much as you can rearrange the other petals to give a good shape. If the paste keeps falling off the wire, try using a firmer paste. Flowers may be dried upside down

to give an open effect, or the wire may be inserted into a piece of Oasis. Pipe your centre after the flower is dry.

Daisy

Method 1

Step 1
Take a piece of paste, make a ball and insert a piece of cotton-covered wire into it. Flatten to give almost a button shape, with a slightly raised and curved centre. This is the centre of your daisy; make several and allow them to dry overnight before using.

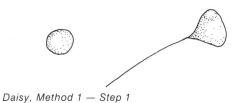

Daisy, Method 1 — Step 1

Step 2
Take another piece of paste and form a ball about 1 cm in diameter. Shape this to a tear drop and then insert your rounded skewer into the centre and hollow it out to a cone. Do not make your cone too fine this time or your petals will fall off when you start to handle them.

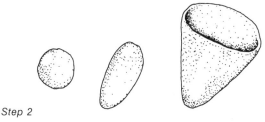

Step 2

Step 3
Cut ten evenly-sized sections deep into the cone. You will need to cut about two thirds down the cone, to allow room for your centre.

Step 3

Step 4
Shape each petal by cutting away excess paste and forming a point at the centre of each petal. Using the pressure of your fingers, pinch and flatten each petal to smooth it out a little, then bend it back a little as you finish.

Step 5
Moisten the inside of the centre and draw through the dry centre you have already made to rest in the middle of the flower. Flatten the base of the flower by pressing gently so that the base and cone of petals are securely attached to each other.

Step 5

Method 2

Step 1
Take a piece of paste, roll it out thinly and cut it to about 3 cm x 15 mm.

Step 2
Take your scalpel and cut ten evenly spaced petals to about half-way down the width. Shape each petal to a point.

Step 3
Moisten the underside of a dry centre (previously made). Wrap this piece of paste around the centre so that it fits snugly. Press the paste under the centre firmly and cut excess paste away. If all your petals do not fit around the centre some can be removed. Bend petals back gently and set aside to dry.

Method 3

There is a variety of cutters, any of which can be used to make daisies. Then may have ten, eight or six petals.

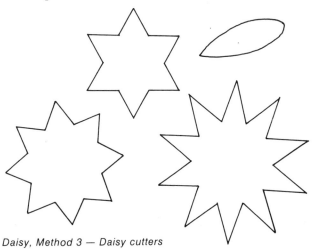

Daisy, Method 3 — Daisy cutters

Step 1
Roll out a piece of paste and cut out a daisy with your cutter.

Step 2
Use a piece of cotton wool or a plastic grape of a suitable size. Place the cut-out shape on a piece of foam and then press the grape or cotton wool into its centre to create a shallow cup effect in the middle.

Step 3
Insert a dry centre by moistening this cut area with a little water and pressing the two together gently. Set aside to dry.

Method 4

Step 1
If a larger flat flower is required, single daisy petal cutters are available. Roll out a piece of paste and cut out a number of petals. Make a few spare ones as they are very fragile.

Step 2
Place the petals into a foil-lined patty tin to give them a gentle curved shape while they dry.

Step 3
When thoroughly dry, pipe a large dot of firm royal icing into the centre of a foil-lined patty tin. Insert your petals in a circle into this icing. Pipe a raised centre of dots with royal icing. Set aside and peel off the flowers when dry.

Calyx

This may be attached by resting the dry flower upside down on some cotton wool. Make and attach your calyx in the same way as for the briar-rose (see page 50). You may prefer to leave these flowers without a calyx as they are very fragile.

The illustrations facing pages 87 and 126 show daisies and flannel flowers. The section on colouring suggests a variety of effects for these flowers.

Grape hyacinth

Grape hyacinths are useful when a touch of blue is needed. These very dainty flowers are particularly suitable for a traditional boy's christening cake. They also make a lovely addition to the flower arrangement facing page 55.

Flower

Step 1
Take a very small piece of paste and insert the handle of a paint brush to form a small shallow bell.

Grape hyacinth — Step 1

Step 2
Insert a long white stamen into the centre and pull it through the flower. Leave just a tip of the stamen showing on the inside of the flower.

Step 2

Step 3
Take an icing bag into which you have placed some royal icing and pipe a row of dots along the rim of the bell.

Step 3

Buds

These are very small, and are made by shaping a small tear drop.

Step 4

Attach several buds and flowers into a cluster about 4 or 5 cm in length. Use florist's tape to attach these to a central piece of wire.

Heath

Heath is a lovely wildflower, usually at its best in winter. It looks bright and cheerful, growing in its multi-coloured splendour in the Victorian countryside. The most common colour is pink but it can also be red, white or cream. The heath seen on the decorated plate facing page 38 is typical of the most common variety.

Flower

Step 1
Make a piece of paste the size of a pea. Work it to a long tubular shape, from 10 to 15 mm long.

Step 2
Insert the handle of your paint brush or, if that is too thick, a fine wooden skewer, into the paste and work to a fine tubular shape, just a little wider at the top.

Heath — Step 2

Step 3
Make five very shallow cuts into the top of this flower no deeper than 3 mm. Cut away excess paste and form five pointed petals.

Step 4
Pull these petals out from the flower and fine them down between the fingers. Depending on which variety you wish to make, check to see if your flower requires stamens. Many varieties do not have stamens; some have only one long stigma for which you can use a plain stamen cotton. The flowers on the plate facing page 38 have four stamens.

Step 5
Insert a stamen into the flower; pull it through until it is just visible at the base of the flower. Pinch at the base to ensure the flower is attached. Set aside to dry.

Step 5

Buds

These are made by shaping a small piece of paste to a long tubular shape and attaching a stamen cotton.

Heath bud

Calyx

The heath calyx is very small so it is best painted on.

Leaves

Roll out a piece of paste and cut out a few small, pointed leaves with your scalpel. Attach a stamen cotton to each leaf.

Flowers, buds and leaves may be attached to a central stem with florist's tape.

Completed leaves

Daphne

Daphne is another popular small flower often used by the decorator. It combines well with native or spring flowers (see cake facing page 54). The underside of daphne is the coloured part. It ranges from a musk pink through to a deep maroon.

Daphne may be made either freehand or with a cutter.

Daphne cutters

Flower

Method 1

Step 1
Take a piece of paste the size of a pea and shape to a tear drop. Using the back of your paint brush, hollow the piece out to a cone shape.

Daphne, Method 1 — Step 1

Step 2
Divide into four equal parts, cutting about halfway down into the cone. You may cut off the excess paste to form pointed petals or, using your thumb and forefinger, shape each section to a pointed petal then turn the petals back.

Step 2

Step 3
Push one pair of petals back further than the other pair. Look at a real flower if possible to achieve a realistic effect.

Step 4
Insert one lemon stamen through the centre of the flower until the stamen is only just showing, deep in the centre of the flower. Pinch paste around the base and cut off any excess.

Method 2

Step 1
Roll out a piece of paste to a fine thickness. Cut out several flowers with a cutter. Take one and cover the rest with a plastic lid.

Step 2
Place the flower onto a piece of foam and press down into its centre with the rounded end of your hair curler pin. This will give the flower a cupped shape. Insert one stamen into the centre and pull through. You can take each flower and squeeze it a little between your fingers, to give the crinkled look that most daphne flowers have.

Bud

Daphne buds are made from a small piece of paste attached to the end of a stamen and shaped to a fat point. There are often more buds than flowers in a spray of daphne.

Buds

Leaves

Daphne leaves are dark green, long and firm. You can cut them out freehand with your scalpel. Attach a hooked piece of wire if needed.

Leaves

Calyx

A small calyx may be painted on flowers and buds after they are dry.

Tea-tree flower

These flowers are not very well known as the flowering period for tea-tree is quite short. Each species has a different sized flower as well as different colours. The decorated plate facing page 38 shows a beautiful, large, pink flower. The instructions given here are for the larger variety but you can adjust the directions to make the smaller varieties. The centre will alter depending on which variety you are making.

Flower

Step 1
Take a piece of gum paste the size of a large pea. Using the rounded skewer, hollow out the paste to form a medium size cone.

Tea-tree flower — Step 1

Step 2
Divide this cone into five equal parts. Cut off the excess paste with your sharp pointed scissors so that you are cutting your petals to an even rounded petal shape.

Step 2

Step 3
Make up a centre. (This may be made the day before and allowed to dry.) Take a piece of paste the size of a small pea. Insert a moistened, hooked piece of cotton-covered wire, pinch the base and flatten the top to give a rounded button shape. Place a short rod stamen cotton into this.

Step 3

Step 4
Insert the wire through the centre of the flowers and pull down. Press gently to ensure that it becomes attached. Set aside to dry by pushing the wire into a piece of Oasis.

Buds

Tea-tree buds are fat and rounded. Attach a piece of cotton-covered wire to a small pea size piece of gum paste and colour when the bud is dry.

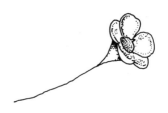

Completed tea-tree flower

Leaves

These are usually slender, though there are some varieties that have a small oval leaf. Cut out the leaves freehand with your scalpel and attach a wire to each one. Vein the centre of each one.

Pittosporum

The pittosporum is another flower which is often overlooked by decorators but its beautiful cream to lemon coloured flowers are most attractive, as shown on the decorated plate facing page 38.

Flower

Step 1
Take a piece of gum paste large enough to make a ball about 1 cm in diameter. Using your rounded skewer, hollow out the ball to a fine cone shape.

Pittosporum — Step 1

Step 2
Cut your cone evenly into five sections about two-thirds of the way down into it. Cut each petal to a long rounded shape and curve back and under a little. Cut away any excess paste.

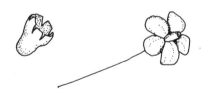

Step 2

Step 3
Make a long stigma, about 10 mm long and 2 mm wide, from another piece of paste.

Step 4
Insert a piece of hooked cotton-covered wire down through the centre of your flower, then pull a little of the paste down from the base of the flower. Ease this against the wire by rolling the wire backwards and forwards between your fingers.

Step 5
Moisten the centre of the flower with a little egg white or water and insert the stigma into this. If the stigma is too large it can be cut back a little with your scissors. The flowers are usually seen in dense, round clusters surrounded by leaves.

Buds

These are the same as for the tea-tree bud.

Leaves

Pittosporum leaves are similar in shape, colour and size to those of Daphne (page 84).

Calyx

A small round of paste attached to the base of the flower is all that is needed.

Lavender

Lavender is always a popular choice for use on cakes for older people. It is also attractive when combined in sprays of pink and mauve flowers.

Flower

Step 1
Make a ball of gum paste about 1 cm in diameter. Roll it out between your fingers to a cylindrical shape 2 cm long, leaving the top end slightly pointed.

Lavender — Step 1

Step 2
Take another piece of paste, roll it out thinly and then cut out pairs of petals freehand. You will need gradually to increase the size of these as you progress down the length of the flower. Smooth and fine down the outer edges of each petal by pressing them between your fingers.

Step 2

Step 3
Attach petals opposite each other using a little water or egg white. Allow the second petal to overlap the outer edge of the first one. Place these petals up to the top of the cylinder so that just a little of the centre bud is showing.

Step 4

Continue making pairs of petals, arranging them so that every other pair has the centre of its petals below an overlap area. Attach five pairs of petals altogether. Cut off excess paste at the base.

Step 4

Step 5

After you have coloured your flower, make a little royal icing in the same colour and pipe small forget-me-nots over the area of over-lapped petals on each row. These may be piped directly or attached when they are dry.

Attach a piece of thick cotton-covered wire at the base of the flower.

Peone rose

The peone roses on the cake facing page 94 are very impressive. Because they are so large you only need a few on one cake.

The flower is made in three stages and some drying time is required between each stage. You first make the bud-like centre, then the crimped petals and finally the outer petals which give this flower its distinctive appearance and height.

Flower

Step 1

Take a large piece of paste, roll it out thinly, then, using three rose cutters, cut out your petals in graded sizes, starting with the smallest. Cut out four small petals and stretch and flute the outer edges with the handle of your paint brush. Assemble them together by brushing a little water or egg white at the base and a little

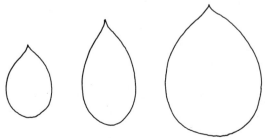

Peone rose — Step 1 (i)

way up the right-hand edge where the petals overlap. Push your petals close together using the back of your brush so that they are close and compact. Part of the base of each of these petals will form the base of the flower.

Step 1 (ii)

Step 2

Cut out four petals using your medium size cutter. Flute the top of these petals. Arrange these around the centre you have just made. These petals are overlapped slightly by moistening the right-hand lower edge of each petal. Tuck the last petal in over the first of the second row of petals.

Step 3

Using your large rose petal cutter, cut out three petals, flute the outer top edges and then attach them to the centre in the same way as the others. You now have a centre made up of three rows of petals. Place this in a foil-lined patty tin to allow to dry. If this does not support your flower sufficiently make a support by folding and pinching a piece of foil to the required size and shape.

Step 4

The next part of your flower consists of the crimped petals. These are very 'crinkly' and very full. Allow for two rows of six petals, though you can include as many as you think look attractive. Roll out more paste to a very fine thickness and cut out your petals. Place the petals you are not working on under a plastic lid. Taking one petal at a time, use your fine scissors to cut the outer edges, giving them a crimpled effect. Gather the petal at the lower

Step 4

Facing: Made by Mrs. Pat Welch, this traditional wedding cake has beautifully-made hyacinths, Cecil Brunner roses and boronia. The extension work and embroidery are soft and delicate, with the same design being embroidered on the pillars as well.

edge and place in a foil-lined patty tin (or just a suitable piece of foil). Make five more petals in this way. Join them together with a little water at the base and at the bottom of the right-hand edge of each petal.

Step 5
Cut out six more petals with your large rose cutter. Attach these petals over the previous layer, allowing more overlap at the centre to make them look a little shorter. Leave to dry. Cut out another twelve petals with your large cutter. This time do not flute or crimp them, just allow them to dry in the patty tin in a cupped shape.

Step 6
Cut out another twelve petals with your large cutter. This time do not flute or crimp them; just allow them to dry in the patty tin in a cupped shape.

Step 7
Pipe a little royal icing between six of the cupped petals and set them into a raised circular shape, with the cupped area on the underside. Pipe enough royal icing in the centre to hold them together.

Step 8
Repeat the process with the other six petals, facing them the opposite way.

Step 9
Pipe several dots of royal icing in the middle and lay the circle of crimped petals over this.

Step 10
Pipe several dots of royal icing on the underside of the centre and attach this on top of the centre of the crimped petals. Press these three layers gently together.

Step 11
Finally lay this three-tiered centre on top of the now dry convex lower layer of petals, having first piped several dots of royal icing on both pieces. Press gently together and allow to dry thoroughly before using.

Facing: This cake has a lovely fresh touch with its clean crisp lines and colours. Mrs Constance Russell has presented daisies, lemon blossoms and forget-me-nots to achieve this effect. The beautiful moulded bells are cleverly arranged with small sprays of these flowers in the top three bells.

Maidenhair Fern

The fern seen in the floral arrangement facing page 38 is lovely and delicate. It is fresh in appearance and has many uses. It is made freehand, so no cutter is required.

Step 1
Fine cotton-covered wire and stamen cottons will be required for this. Wire only may be used if stamen cottons are unavailable.

Colour the wire (or cottons) in either a dark brown or green by inserting into some methylated spirits to which you have added several drops of the required food colour. Lay on a sheet of paper towelling to absorb excess moisture and allow to dry for about five minutes.

Step 2
Use a small quantity of gum paste about the size of a small pea. (This may be left white or else coloured a pale shade of green.) Flatten it out between your fingers.

Maidenhair fern — Step 2

Step 3
Insert the wire by pinching it into the centre of the paste. Allow a little thickness where the wire is inserted so that there is enough support.

Step 3

Step 4
Using small fine scissors, cut the paste into a small leaf shape. It is wise to look at several varieties of this fern to note their various shapes and sizes.

Step 5
Cut small indentations at the base of the leaf. These have almost a zig-zag effect.

Step 6
Finally round the outer edges slightly. Make these up individually and lay them flat to dry.

Step 7
The wires and cottons are then attached together to form sprays. Use brown or green florist's tape to wire the fern together. Make sure the tape is stretched as fine as possible; it

may be cut in half lengthwise to ensure the finest result. Sprays will have to remain small so that they do not break apart because of their weight.

Step 7

The most effective colouring for this fern is achieved by using a variety of green pastels. The scraped powder may be brushed on dry. A combination of pale and dark green may be used. A little brown is also suitable for the variegated variety. There are many ferns which may be made in this way, depending on which type you require. Some of the long-leaf ones may have to be adapted to reduce breakages.

Christmas bell

These flowers are very attractive for any cake which requires red in its colour scheme. They are popular for use on Christening cakes. See examples of this flower on the cake facing page 126.

Flower

Step 1
Flowers are made freehand, so you will not require a cutter. Take a piece of paste about 1 cm in diameter. Using the rounded end of a skewer, insert it into the ball of paste and hollow it out to form a bell shape. If your skewer sticks to the paste, dip it into cornflour occasionally. Your flower can be just a little thicker than most, because these flowers have a rough rippled surface on the outside. Do not make them too thick.

Christmas bell — Step 1

Step 2
Allow your flowers to have almost a pointed shape at the base, and allow a little extra thickness there to support the flower after you insert the wire. Using your fine small scissors, make six cuts into the top of the cone, only about 5 mm deep.

Step 2

Step 3
Cut each of these petals to a point by cutting off all the corners, then squeeze and pinch the petals into a pointed shape.

Step 3

Step 4
Insert a piece of hooked cotton-covered wire down through the centre of the flower and pinch the base to secure it. Six stamens, no longer than the length of the flower, should be inserted while the gum paste is still moist enough to hold them in place. These flowers may be dried upside down, or they may be allowed to dry in an upturned egg carton.

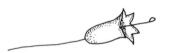

Step 4

No leaves or calyx are required.

Buds

Step 1
The buds are quite fat and almost as long as the flowers. Take a larger piece of paste, moisten the hooked end of a piece of cotton-covered wire with a little water and insert this into one end.

Step 2
Roll the other end between the fingers until you have a long tubular shape just a little shorter than your flowers. The top part of the bud is a little fatter than the rest.

Step 3
Using either the scalpel or the fine scissors, make a few line indentations at the top of the bud and then allow it to dry.

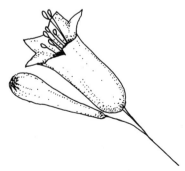

Completed Christmas bell

Christmas bush

These flowers are another favourite for native flower arrangements. They are a little smaller than Christmas bells and have only five petals.

Flowers

Step 1

Take a piece of gum paste the size of a large pea. Using either the rounded end of your paint brush or the end of a skewer, insert it into the middle and hollow the paste out to a cone shape.

Step 2

Cut the top into five and then shape each section to a pointed petal. The petals are cut down about one-third of the length of the cone.

Step 3

Insert a moistened hooked piece of cotton-covered wire down through the centre of the flower. Pull it down to the base and then pinch to secure the wire firmly.

Christmas bush — Step 3

Step 4

Curve the petals out gently, and add a few short stamen cottons close together at the bottom.

Buds

Buds are made by rolling a small quantity of paste onto a piece of wire and shaping to a small rounded end.

Buds

No calyx is required for this flower.

Leaves

These are a little different from the usual because they are made up of three sections. They are best made freehand, and the serrations can be made by using the back of a scalpel blade. After cutting out the leaf, mark out veins and then press the edge of your blade along all the outer edges to give a serrated effect. Dry the leaves draped over pencils or skewers, or use pieces of foil, to allow the leaf some curves and twists. Attach a moistened hooked piece of wire while paste is still moist.

Completed Christmas bush

Wattle

Wattle or mimosa is always a bright addition to a spray of flowers. It is very effective and yet quite simple to make. Wattle is seen in many sizes, shapes and colours, so you may adapt it to suit your needs. Again, it would be a good idea to check a few samples of the real flowers for accuracy.

Flowers

Step 1

Take a sufficient quantity of gum paste to make the number of wattle stems that you will require. Colour this either a deep lemon or a bright yellow, making sure that your colour is kneaded in well. Any of the types of colours are suitable for this.

Step 2

Mould several balls from this paste. A variety of sizes will be needed, but they should not be too large or too small. If you intend to make the longer tubular variety of wattle, shape your paste accordingly.

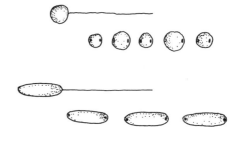

Wattle — Step 2

Step 3

Make some of these balls with a piece of hooked cotton-covered wire inserted into the centre.

Step 4
Using a piece of plain wire, make a hole through each ball so that they can be threaded together after they dry. When dry, thread several balls together in varying numbers. Use the smaller ones at the tip. These stems of wattle can be used singly or in clusters.

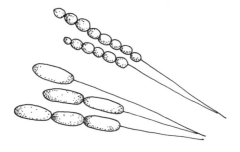

Step 4

Step 5
The stems may be brushed with water or egg white and then dipped into lemon-coloured castor sugar to give a realistic effect. Castor sugar can be coloured by adding a few drops of yellow food colouring. Mix and then place in a tepid oven to dry before use. Alternatively, the wattle may be dipped into the castor sugar before each ball is assembled. Tubular wattle may be made singly, with one piece only attached to a piece of wire, or with two or three pieces together. No buds, calyx or leaves are needed.

Gum nuts

Gum nuts are very much an Australian feature on a cake, and look very attractive combined with Australian wild flowers. They are also very welcome as an ornament on a boy's cake. A spray of gum nuts and gum leaves, with perhaps just a few of the appropriate eucalyptus flowers, is very striking. Gum nuts are seen on a variety of eucalyptus trees and range from very small to about 3 cm in length. They are seen after the tree has finished flowering, although both nuts and flowers are sometimes seen together for a short period of time. These gum nuts may be made in two ways. The method chosen depends on the size required.

Small gum nuts

Step 1
Take a small piece of paste about the size of a pea. Using the rounded end of a paint brush, push it into the centre and slightly hollow it out to a small cone shape. Note that your cone is not

meant to be thin, and that often the outer part of the cone is best left a little thicker to give a cup shape.

Step 2
Insert a moistened piece of hooked cotton-covered wire down through the centre. Pinch the base to secure the wire and allow to dry. These gum nuts can be coloured in green or brown, or a combination of the two colours. Wire together with florist's tape to make up small sprays.

Small gum nuts — Step 2

Large gum nuts

Step 1
Take a ball of paste, and mould this to a slightly oval shape.

Step 2
If a stem is required, use a very thick cotton-covered wire. Hook one end and insert this at one of the longer ends.

Step 3
Use the end of a knitting needle, or any other suitable tool. Insert the fat end of the needle into the pointed end of the oval shaped paste. Push this through the paste for about 5-7 mm in depth. Re-shape the paste to retain an oval shape.

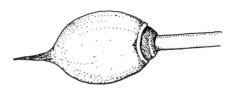

Large gum nuts — Step 3

Step 4
Using the pointed part of the needle, insert the needle into the paste to form four holes in the depression made already. For gum nuts which are smaller, take the ball of paste and hollow it out with the back of the needle, using the fat base to give the nut its bulging shape. Allow the cone shape to remain a little thick at the outer edges. Insert wire if required.

Step 4

Leaves

Gum leaves vary in size, but they all have a similar shape. Cut these out freehand, but scale them to a size suitable for your needs. Do not forget to drape leaves over the handle of a wooden spoon or to twist them so that they dry in a variety of natural shapes. Mark out veins with the back of a scalpel blade and attach a moistened piece of cotton-covered wire which has been hooked at one end.

Leaves

Flowers

Step 1
These may be made by shaping a piece of paste to the gum nut stage. Insert a piece of wire as described for the gum nut.

Step 2
Cut several pieces of red stamen cottons to about 1 cm lengths. Using a pair of tweezers,

insert these into the outer rim of the cup-shaped gum nut while it is still moist. Look at a real flower to see how to place these cottons. Insert one long stamen in the centre for the stigma. Your cottons may be gently curved before they are used to give a softer effect.

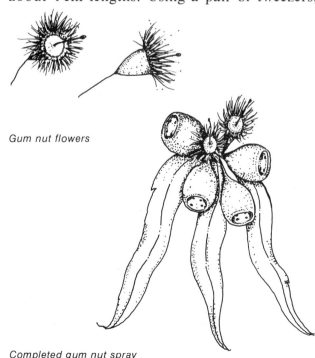

Gum nut flowers

Completed gum nut spray

Waratah

The waratah can be a lovely focal point on a cake. However, it needs to be well made to look realistic, and is generally made much smaller than the real flower. It is not recommended for use on very small cakes.

Flower

These flowers are usually red with slight touches of green or brown towards the centre. Some reds are difficult to achieve, so these flowers may be made by colouring the paste with red food colouring powder before moulding. Another method is to colour the paste a dark shade of pink and then recolour after the flower is dry. Choose whichever method you prefer, or perhaps try making them in white and then colour two or three times to get a rich full tone.

Step 1
Take a large ball of gum paste 15-20 mm in diameter. Shape this so that the top is slightly raised and curved and the lower part is almost flat with a soft curve at the edges. This is the flower centre. It should be allowed to dry for two or three days before it is used. To assist in drying, use a skewer, hat pin or toothpick and push it into the base of this ball, making several holes to allow faster drying. You may wish to attach a very strong, thick cotton-covered wire to the base, or a toothpick may do just as well. Whichever you choose, it will have to support the weight of your flower.

Waratah — Step 1

Step 2
After your centre has dried, make a piping bag and insert a No. 1 writing tube. Fill the bag using either white or red royal icing and then pipe a series of dots on the ball. Start at the top

of the centre. Pipe your first dot in the centre, then pipe a row of dots around this. Place your second row of dots between the dots in the row above. Follow this pattern until you have covered about three quarters of the ball. Gradually increase the size of the dots so that they are larger as you progress down the ball. Allow the lower dots to drag down a little so that they are almost a comma shape. Allow to dry thoroughly.

Step 2

Step 3
Use three graded cutters or cut out your petals freehand. You will need seven to nine petals in each row.

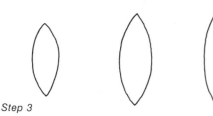

Step 3

Petals may be made, allowed to dry, and then attached with a little egg white or a small amount of royal icing. If this method is used, place petals over a wooden spoon to dry, or shape several pieces of foil to the required curve to rest the petals on while they dry.

Step 4
There are three rows of petals placed around the centre. The first row remains very close to the centre, the next is placed a little further away, and the outside ones are placed slanting out. They may be pinched at the points and twisted or bent a little to give a realistic effect.

Step 4

Step 5
Petals may also be attached while they are moist. Brush a little water or egg white on the underside of the centre, then gently press the

petal to attach. Curve the outer petals back as required. The petals in your first row may overlap a little. The points on all the petals may be pinched together at the tip. Outer petals may also be twisted a little when they are attached. It may be easier to allow time for drying after attaching each row of petals.

No calyx is required.

Leaves

Leaves will probably not be required either. A large leaf in the shape of a fatter petal is the closest replica you will need. The leaves of the waratah are very stiff and serrated, so allow for this when you shape them. Make serrations with the back of a scalpel blade. Mark out veins with this also.

Bud

If a bud is required, it is best to make it as a whole flower with all or most of the petals hugging the centre to give a closed effect. Most arrangements, however, do not require buds.

Holly

Leaves

These are a very traditional decoration used on Christmas cakes. The leaves are very strong, dark and shiny. There is also a variegated variety.

Step 1
These leaves may be made by cutting out from a piece of rolled out gum paste, either freehand or with a cutter. They may also be made by placing the paste over a real leaf or a plastic one. If these are to be used it is best to cut off the sharp points and to rub a little cornflour over the upper surface of the leaf, that is, the side with the veins showing.

Holly — Step 1

Step 2
Using your fingers, rub off the excess paste at the edges and press down a little firmer over the veined ridges. Ensure that the outer edges are smooth. Allow these leaves to set for a couple of minutes and then remove by peeling back the

leaf from the paste. If you would like more twists or curves, allow them to dry over a handle or place foil to support them in the required shape. Leaves which have been made freehand can be veined with the back of a scalpel blade and then allowed to dry in a similar way. Insert wire if required.

Berries

These are lovely and bright. They are made by inserting a moistened hooked piece of cotton-covered wire into a ball of paste. The paste may be coloured first by using a little red powder food colouring. Both berries and leaves may be made in a variety of sizes. Florist's tape can also be used to make up into sprays.

Holly berries

Stephanotis

Stephanotis is a very popular flower for weddings, because of its beautiful fragrance. It is often requested for the wedding cake to complement the bridal bouquet. This flower in reality is quite a long specimen. You may wish to adapt its length according to your needs. The stephanotis used on the cake between pages 94-95 is quite small. I am giving instructions on how to make this flower according to the size I prefer. Try making it in two or three different lengths before making a final choice.

Flower

Step 1
The length of my completed flower is approximately 2 cm. Take a piece of gum paste the size of a large pea. Roll this between your fingers until you have made a long tear-shaped cone about 1½ cm in length.

Stephanotis — Step 1

Step 2
Using the handle of your paint brush, insert it into the fatter part of the cone and hollow out about 7 mm of the top.

Step 3
Cut this section into five parts and then cut off the corners to form five pointed petals. Pinch and press each of these petals to give a softer look and then fold them out almost flat. Ensure that the base of the cone is small and pointed so that it will fit into a calyx.

Step 3

Buds

The buds for this flower are easily made, and give the spray a realistic effect. Start with a piece of paste the same size as for the flower; this time, however, after you roll the paste between the fingers to create a tear-shaped cone, squeeze the paste a little at the centre so that you form a rounded bubble at the top. Shape the top to a slightly pointed ball.

Calyx

The calyx of this flower makes it look distinctive; it is just a small replica of the flower.

Step 1
To make a calyx take a smaller piece of gum paste, hollow it out to a cone and shape five sepals of equal size. Pinch each one to a point.

Step 2
Using the handle of your paint brush, make the hollow in the centre the right size to fit your flower into.

Step 3
Moisten the inside of the calyx. Insert a hooked piece of cotton-covered wire down through the centre, and then insert the base end of your flower into this so that the wire is attached to both the calyx and the flower. If your flower appears to need more support, push the wire up through the lower part of it while it is still moist.

Calyx

No leaves are required.

More decorative ideas

Marzipan fruits and vegetables

Fruits and vegetables are very realistic and easy to make. They make a lovely gift presented in a small perspex box. Small patty papers are available for this use. A cluster of them can also be used as a decoration on a cake.

The size of your fruit or vegetables will depend on personal choice and on whether they are to be used on a cake or not. Remember to make your items to scale so that your selection looks well proportioned together.

Cloves or washed dry fruit stems can be inserted to add a realistic look. All items should be coloured when they are completely dry.

Apple

Take a ball of marzipan of a suitable size. Give it a gentle curve with your hands. If the apple is to be a delicious variety, give it a slightly pointed effect at the bottom. Make small indentations at the top and bottom. A small piece of a dry clean stalk or stem may be added if the apple is small. If it is large, cut a clove in half and push the long end into the top and the other part into the base. Paint with undiluted food colours of your choice. Add a little lemon or brown to the green to soften its tone.

Apricot

Use a suitably sized piece of paste and smooth it between your palms to give a realistic look. Add a stem or clove and colour when dry. Orange with a slight touch of lemon or green will be needed.

Avocado

Shape to suit size. No stems are required. Paint in dark shades of green or purple.

Baby squash

Baby squash is very effective. Take a ball and flatten it a little between the palms. Give a slight pull and twist at the top to represent the stalk. Use the end of a paint brush to form slight depressions in the side of the rim. Paint very pale green.

Banana

These are easy to make by rolling a piece of marzipan into a thin sausage shape. Bend slightly to curve, and then pinch the ends to slight points. Paint yellow with spots or streaks of brown or green. Add stalks if needed.

Canteloupe

This can be made in the same way as the pumpkin, but colour the outside caramel and green.

Carrot

Take a ball and roll one end between your fingers so that it tapers to a narrower point. Use the end of a skewer to form a small hole where the leaves have been cut off. Mark small indentations and lines along the length where required. Paint orange with a few brown specks.

Facing, above: This unusual cake has a lovely arrangement of peone roses, hyacinths, lavender and freesias. Made by Mrs Mary Medway, this is an example of traditional work presented in a refreshingly different way.

Centre: Made by Mrs Shirley Vass, this is a superb collection of bell cakes decorated with phalaenopsis orchids. This prize-winning cake has been beautifully presented. The orchids and carriage placed on the board add to the composition.

Cauliflower

This can be made in sections. Take several small balls of marzipan and press them over the surface of a sieve or in a piece of tulle. Attach together with a little royal icing. Separate leaves may be moulded and attached, or leave the centre white and paint the underside green to represent leaves.

Cherry

A cherry is just a small ball with a small depression where the stem should be. Wash and

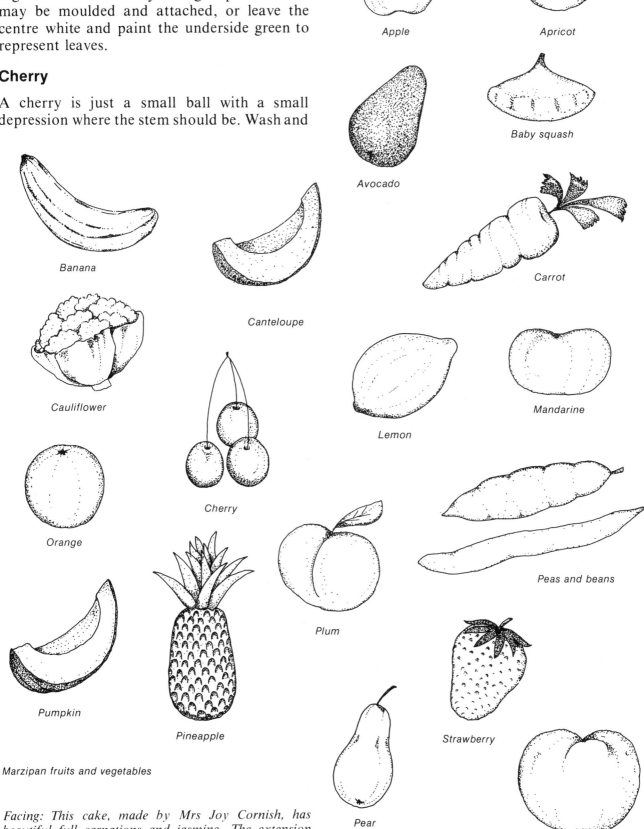

Marzipan fruits and vegetables

Apple

Apricot

Avocado

Baby squash

Banana

Canteloupe

Carrot

Cauliflower

Lemon

Mandarine

Orange

Cherry

Pumpkin

Pineapple

Plum

Peas and beans

Pear

Strawberry

Tomato

Facing: This cake, made by Mrs Joy Cornish, has beautiful full carnations and jasmine. The extension border is double layered, and the tiny prayer book has a flooded cover with lace inserts.

dry the real stems during the cherry season so that they may be stored and used when needed. Leave double stems attached together. Just trim the base a little when they are to be used. Colour with red.

Lemon

Start with a ball and pinch out two slight points at each end. Colour lemon and green.

Mandarine

Shape a ball to a flatter shape between the palms. Add a stem and ripple the surface over a grater. Colour orange when dry.

Orange

Use the same technique as for the mandarine but allow it to remain round. Colour the same.

Pear

Take a ball of marzipan. Pull up a piece from one end so that a pear shape is formed. Flatten the base a little if required. Insert a stem and base end. Colour green, yellow or brown.

Peas and beans

Roll a piece of marzipan to a thin sausage and pinch off at both ends. Make slight indentations with a paint brush handle to give the effect of peas in the pod. Colour green when dry. Beans can be made in the same way as peas, but flatten the sausage shape a little first.

Pineapple

This is made in two sections. Shape one piece of marzipan to a cylindrical shape. Smooth out the top and lower edges. Make markings with a grater. Using your round skewer, make a deep hole in the top. Take another piece of marzipan and shape to a cone. Hold it with the fat part facing down. Using your small scissors, make small cuts into the cone in a circular pattern. Cut each row between the two previous 'leaves' so that you are creating the top leaves. Practice will perfect this method. After all leaves have been cut, turn the cone up the other way and make one or two more cuts into the top. Use a skewer to push leaves down and out to give a better effect and to separate them. Dip your scissors in cornflour as needed, to prevent marzipan sticking to them. Attach the pieces together with egg white or water, making the

hole larger if needed. Colour pieces separately or together. The top is green and the base can be yellow, orange and green.

Plum

These can be made like the apricot. Flatten them slightly and then, using your skewer, mark a line from the centre to the bottom along one side only. Paint with raspberry red and a little blue if needed.

Pumpkin

A slice of pumpkin may be a better size than a whole one. Shape a piece of marzipan to a large wedge and allow the inside to be scooped out. Colour the outside green and the inside a light orange.

Strawberry

Take a ball of marzipan. Pull slightly at the base to give a rounded, longer look. Pinch a little at the top. They may be painted red or a full strength rose pink. Roll them into sugar while they are still wet, so that the attached sugar will give a more realistic effect. Pipe one or two green leaves with royal icing after they are dry.

Tomato

Make these almost the same as the mandarine, allowing for the fact that they are a little fatter. Make indentations at the top and a little way down the sides. Paint red with a small splash of green in places.

Zucchini, potatoes, cabbage and eggplant can also be made from marzipan. Try several of these and experiment with colour to achieve the most realistic effects.

Sugar and non-sugar ornaments

Cone people and other sugar novelties

There are many occasions when 'people', novelties or sugar ornaments are needed to decorate a cake. Children will love these items on a birthday cake and take great pleasure in keeping their decorations to show friends. There are many other special occasions when sugar ornaments are preferable to flowers, such as church occasions, sporting events and male birthdays or retirement celebrations. You could use a box of carpenter's tools for a carpenter or handyman, a barrow of fruit and vegetables for a greengrocer, or a swaggie hat, fishing line and tackle box for a keen fisherman. These are only a few suggestions. Time and imagination will provide you with many novel ideas.

Moulded novelties can be made from left-over scraps of plastic or almond icing and from gum paste. Ensure that your paste or icing is firm enough to hold its shape. You may need to knead in extra icing or cornflour to make it stiffer. Tragacanth gum powder may also be added to allow for quicker drying. Knead one tablespoon per 500 g of plastic icing or gum paste. Royal icing is used for special features.

Father Christmas

Step 1
From pink moulding paste to which a touch of brown has been added, make the head (with eyes, nose and mouth) on a toothpick. First pinch a little of the paste forward for the nose and hollow out the eyes slightly with a skewer. Press gently around the mouth to shape it and the chin. Fine detail is not necessary as the aim is to create an overall impression. Set the head aside to dry.

Step 2
Now make the shoes by starting with two small balls of black or brown paste and shaping them into two oblongs. Insert half a toothpick in each, the point facing upwards, and set them aside to dry.

Step 3
Form the cone for the body from red paste and cut it at an acute upward angle for the arms. Mould the arms while the paste is still wet and then position them as you wish.

Step 4
Attach the head to the body by pushing the toothpick into it. Then attach the body to the shoes by pushing down onto the half-toothpicks. Set aside to dry, propping up if necessary.

Step 5
Add the hat and then pipe a pompon into its tip. Pipe the beard, eyebrows, buttons, trims, etc.

Step 6
As a final touch, trim a sugar cube to look like a parcel and place it in position in Father Christmas's hands with a touch of royal icing.

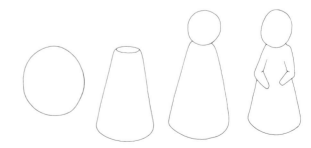

Body for Mother and Father Christmas and the angel

Father Christmas's hat

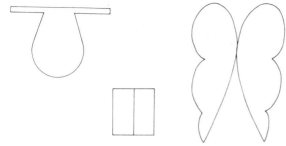

Apron, book and wings

Mother Christmas

Do the same as for Father Christmas, but make an apron from a piece of white paste trimmed as required. Using a small writing tube, pipe lines of icing from her forehead to the back of her head for her hair, and then form a bun. Paint a pair of spectacles onto her nose. You could also give her a parcel to hold.

Angel

The procedure here is the same as for that for the Christmas figures, but you need not make feet.

Attach wings to the back with royal icing. Add a book or harp made out of paste or piped in royal icing. A halo can also be piped with royal icing and painted gold or silver. Add hair with royal icing in a small writing tube.

Christmas mice

Each mouse is made in two parts — the body and the head. The back and front legs are cut out, while the tail is a thin roll of paste cut from the back of the body and curved.

The head is made from a ball. The left ear is formed by taking the paste between the left thumb and forefinger and dragging the paste to the left and backwards. The right ear is formed in the same way, using the right thumb and forefinger.

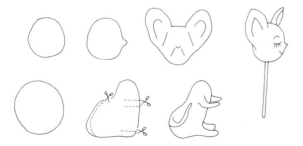

Christmas mice

The mouth and nose are shaped so as to protrude slightly and the nose is tipped up. Use either food colouring or royal icing for the eyes

and features. Add trimmings or accessories as you fancy. You might let each mouse hold a present or some holly and give each one a little red Christmas cap.

Pigs

Each pig is made from a single ball of paste as shown, and the legs, ears and tail are cut as shown. The nose is marked with two small holes. The eyes are painted on with food colouring. Add a little hat if you wish Mr Pig to look a little more debonair.

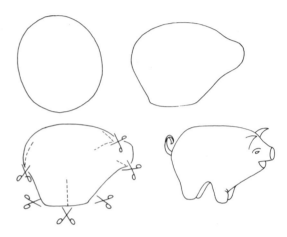

Pigs

Elephants

The shape of your elephant need not be complicated. As long as you accentuate his most significant features — his trunk and big ears — he can be made to look very appealing.

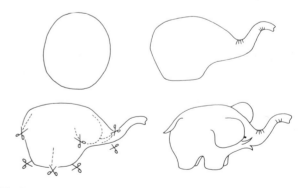

Elephants

Birds

Shape the head, body and tail from one ball of paste as shown in the sketch.

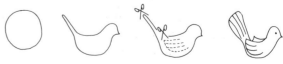

Birds

Snowman

Here again, simplicity is the key. Roll a ball of paste and then roll another smaller one for the head. Add flattened balls of black, brown or blue paste for the eyes, and red ones for the nose and buttons down the front of the body. The mouth is a small red roll.

If you wish, make a small paste 'carrot' for the nose. Make a hat from a flat paste circle with a crown from a flattened ball of paste. Add a little green paste 'feather'. Add a green paste tie with white royal icing dots.

Let your snowman hold a broom too, if you wish.

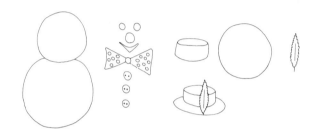

Snowman

Fairies

Step 1
First make the wings from paste, using a small plain leaf cutter, and allow them to dry.

Step 2
To make the body, roll a ball of paste into a cylinder with one end narrower than the other. At the wide end, pinch the paste to a point in the centre to make the neck. Cut the arms and legs with scissors as shown. Position the arms and legs as desired. Let this dry thoroughly.

Step 3
Roll a ball for the head and attach it to the body with egg white or a little royal icing when still wet.

Step 4
Allow the head to dry on the body and then pipe hair in royal icing and attach the wings. Add eyes, nose and mouth with royal icing or by painting them on with food colouring. Clothes may be added if you wish.

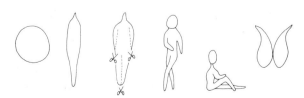

Fairies

Simple clowns

These are based on the same principle as the snowman.

Step 1
First cut a circle of coloured moulding paste or plastic icing as a base.

Step 2
Add a ball of white or coloured paste for the body.

Step 3
Now attach some coloured paste cut with a flower cutter for a collar. The parts may be joined together with egg white or royal icing.

Step 4
Add a ball of icing for the head.

Step 5
The arms are a roll of paste cut into two and attached to the body. Add a small cone of paste for the hat.

Step 6
Do the buttons, eyes, nose, mouth and pompons with royal icing or moulding paste.

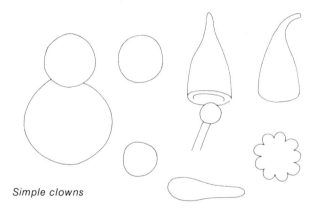

Simple clowns

Clown candle-holders

Step 1

Roll a piece of pale pink moulding paste into a ball a little bigger than a small marble. Dip one end of a toothpick into egg white and insert it into what will be the back of the head of the clown. Allow this to dry thoroughly. Then paint the faces in food colouring.

Step 2
Add the clown's hat, which is a cone of paste, by attaching it to the head with egg white. Make a hole in the top of the hat with a small birthday candle.

Step 3
Using royal icing, pipe eyes, nose, mouth and

then pompons down the front of the hat. You can also add a ruffle (of paste or royal icing, using a petal tube), attaching it to the head with royal icing.

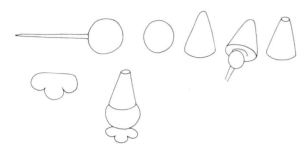

Clown candle-holders

Seals

These are made of plastic icing or marzipan. Start with a ball, roll it into an elongated shape, mould the head and then cut the fins and flippers. Position them as required.

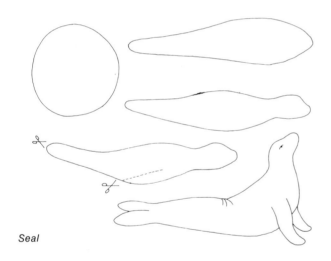

Seal

Toadstool houses

The stem is a thickish roll of paste. The top is a ball of paste shaped by flattening the base and slightly hollowing it. The chimney is a small roll of paste to which a pointed top is added. Windows and doors are thin pieces of paste cut

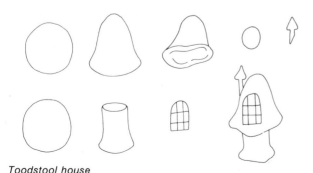

Toodstool house

to shape and painted where necessary. Faces and more house features may be painted on these toadstools with food colouring.

After you have gained experience with these items you may wish to try your own ideas for other novelties.

Sugar moulding

This is one of the simplest of cake decorating techniques, but again, one which produces delightful results.

Moulding sugar

For recipe see page 129. Press the sugar mixture into a mould, place your tile against the open part of the mould, turn it over and then gently remove the mould.

Colouring: When coloured sugar is needed, colour the water before adding it to the sugar.

Bells

Step 1

The bell mould is filled with the sugar mixture (which must be firmly packed). Turn it out immediately and allow it to dry or bake it on a wooden board for five minutes in a low oven. The smaller the bell, the less time will be needed for the sugar to dry.

Making sugar bells — Step 1 (i)

Step 2

Gently lift the sugar bell in your left hand and then, using a small spoon, hollow out the inside of the bell until it is 3-4 mm thick. If you wish, put the bell back into the mould while you hollow it out. Set the bell aside carefully to dry thoroughly.

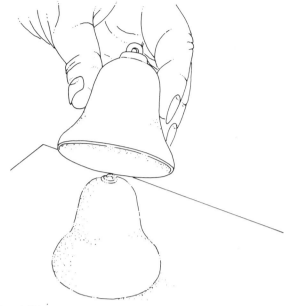

Step 1 (ii)

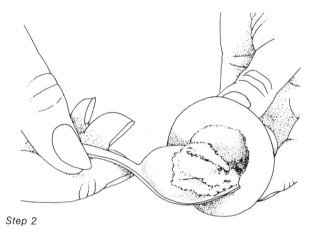

Step 2

Step 3

Using royal icing and a fine writing tube, decorate the outside and/or edge of the bell with dots, lines or scallops.

Children's sand moulds can be used very successfully in sugar moulding, as can any other odd hollow objects around the house.

Pastillage or gum paste ornaments

Pastillage, or gum paste, is a sugar medium used for architectural structures, furniture and any other items which need to be fairly rigid. Over the years, recipes for pastillage have changed and the one I have found most successful is royal icing to which gum tragacanth and extra icing sugar have been added, worked into a dough.

Using the correct knife for cutting out

pastillage pieces is very important and makes the difference between a well and a poorly finished article. A hobby knife or scalpel is ideal for this purpose.

Working with pastillage or gum paste

Roll out the pastillage on a level surface on cornflour. A tile or glass is best for working on, as it is level and can be moved without actually touching or disturbing the pieces already cut.

Lift the pastillage constantly as you roll to make sure that it is not sticking. If necessary, add more cornflour. Always lift the pastillage immediately before cutting it and dust the tile with more cornflour.

Allow the pieces to dry, turning them over every now and then. To do this, place another tile or stiff board over them, turn it over and then remove the first tile. Small pieces may be lifted with an egg lifter or spatula or even gently by hand.

Keep the part of the pastillage where you are not cutting covered with plastic sheeting.

If your pastillage keeps sticking, it is either too moist (in which case add more icing sugar) or else there is not enough cornflour on the rolling surface.

Soft royal icing can be added to the pastillage if it dries and worked in until the pastillage is again pliable.

Cradle

Step 1

Break off some pastillage and roll it out to a 2 mm thickness. To test for thickness, make a cut close to the edge.

Step 2

Place a tracing of the pattern pieces on top of it. Cut carefully around the pattern pieces — three of the 'base' and two of the end piece. Remove the excess pastillage and add it to the main portion in the plastic bag. Turn the pieces over immediately.

Step 3

Leave them to dry and turn them over again after a few hours. If any of the edges are rough or uneven, sand with fine grain sandpaper or an emery board.

Step 4

Place the base of the cradle on a matchbox to raise it. Fill a small writing tube with royal icing and pipe a line on the two short edges of the base. Attach an end piece to each of these edges.

Step 5
Pipe royal icing on the edges of the side pieces, leaving the top edge clear. Then position the side pieces.

Step 6
Allow the cradle to dry thoroughly. Support with cotton wool to hold pieces in place.

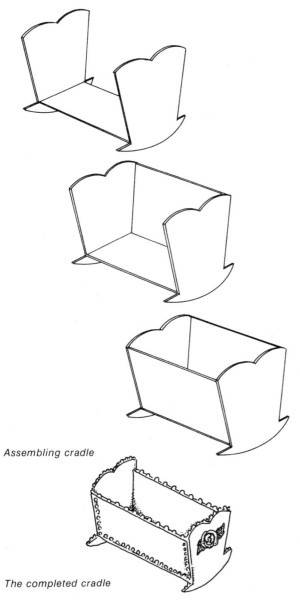

Assembling cradle

The completed cradle

Step 7
Using royal icing and a small writing tube, make a row of beading along each joint and along the top edges of the cradle.

Step 8
Stiffen a little royal icing and colour it green. Fill a sharply pointed plain cone and cut it into the shape for small leaves.

Step 9
Attach small flowers to the outside of the cradle ends with royal icing. Add a few small royal icing leaves to complete the decoration.

If you wish, you may decorate the cradle ends and sides with royal icing embroidery rather than with flowers.

Put a little plastic doll or, if you like, a baby's head made from your flower moulding paste or plastic icing, into the cradle and make a cot cover and pillow from plastic icing.

Birdbath

Step 1
Break off some pastillage and roll it into a ball about the size of a golfball. Flatten one side and shape the other side to a rounded point as shown in the sketch to form the base of the birdbath. Sometimes a small bell may be suitable for this use. Allow to dry on a flat surface dusted with cornflour.

Base

Step 2
Roll out a piece of pastillage on cornflour to a thickness of 2-3 mm. Cut out a scalloped circle (see sketch) with your biscuit cutter and place it inside a patty pan or similar shape, dusted with cornflour. Allow to dry.

Bowl

Step 3
When both base and bowl are thoroughly dry, do Cornelli work with royal icing, using a small or fine writing tube, over the base and on the underside of the bowl.

Facing: There is a great amount of detail in this cake made by Mrs Heather Oswin. The colours and embroidery in the bed quilt and clothes are very appealing. The tired, sick mouse and her anxious visitor are sweet and original. The bed is made of a cake as are the mice. The body of the visiting mouse was baked in three parts. A great deal of time and planning has gone into this charming cake.

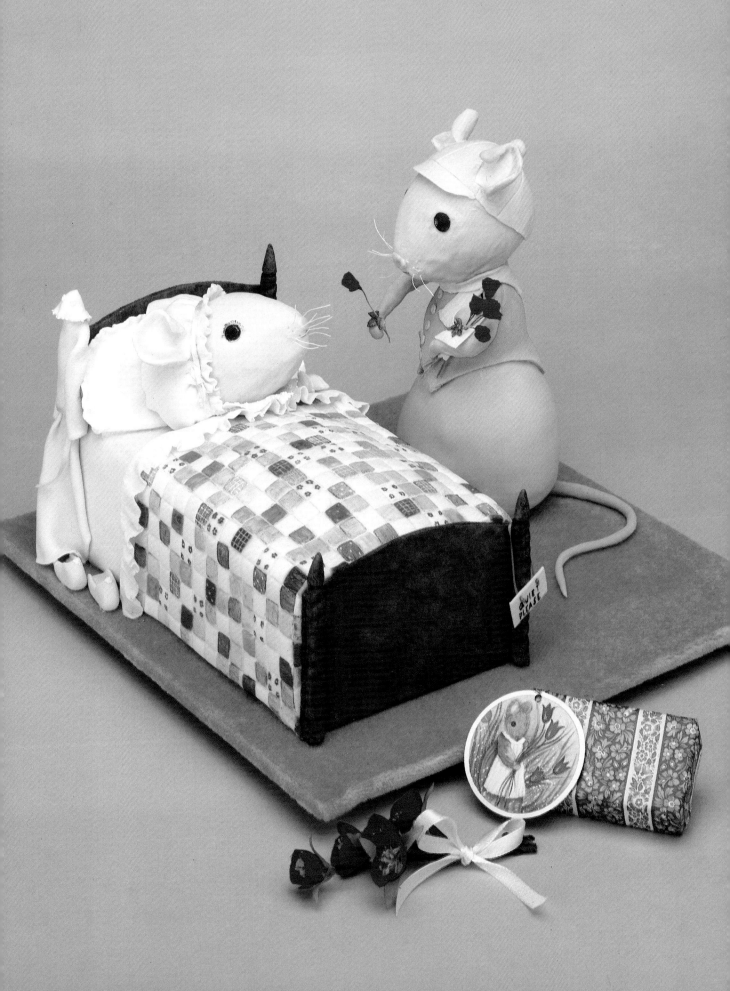

Step 4
Attach the bowl to the base with royal icing and, when dry, add a few royal icing flowers or two little birds.

Birdbath

Plaques

Cut a variety of plaques using cutters or cardboard shapes. Plaques can be kept on hand and decorated as necessary for seasonal cakes, novelties, nameplates on cakes, etc. Small plaques, for example, may be cut for white Easter eggs, or decorated for Christmas cakes, or even used simply as a small token for someone. If you have a patterned rolling pin, this can be used very effectively on your plaques.

Individual place card holders are easily made from the shapes provided below. After these little plaques are dry, attach supports to the back of each one. A small length of pastillage rolled out to the width of a pencil can be attached to the back with a little royal icing. Pipe a line all around the edge of each holder using a soft royal icing at writing consistency. Pipe a double line two thirds of the way down

Place card holders

Facing: This cake would delight any child. It was made by Mrs Nola Cordell. The body consists of two cakes attached together and supported with a piece of dowel. The clothes are all made of sugar, including the shoes. Colours have been used in strong tones to help create the bright, cheerful air of a circus. The board has also been given an unusual treatment with coloured coconut.

the holder to support name cards. These cards can be attached with two or three dots of icing. A small decoration or piped flower may be attached to the top left or right corner to finish.

Moulded bell

Moulded bells made from gum paste or pastillage are often requested as a decoration on wedding cakes. Suitable bell moulds made of plaster of paris, wood or plastic are available from cake decorating supply stores and some large department stores. If these are unavailable, a suitably shaped sherry or wine glass may be used as a substitute.

Step 1
Using a liberal amount of cornflour, dust your mould as evenly as possible. Set aside while you roll out a piece of gum paste or pastillage. Your gum paste should be pliable and just a little soft to allow for plenty of stretching. On the other hand, do not have your paste too soft, or it will become tacky with handling and stick to the inside of your mould.

Step 2
Roll out a suitable amount of paste to about 2 mm in thickness. Now take the paste and gently ease the piece into the mould. Start at the centre of the paste and gently push this down to the base of the bell. If it is an extra deep bell, lightly fold your paste into quarters and then press the base corner down to the base of the bell. Open out the rest of the paste so that it is lying gently against the sides of the bell. Push and gently ease your paste against the sides and at the same time keep turning the bell mould in your left hand. Do not press too hard, or your fingers will work right through the paste and make a hole in the sides.

Moulded bell — Step 2

Step 3
Continue in this way, working up the entire length of the bell, until you come right up to the outer edges. Smooth this down to the bell's edge, then cut off excess paste with a sharp knife. Indent a pattern along the edge if you wish. Some leather tools can be successful for this, or any kitchen item with a fancy edge.

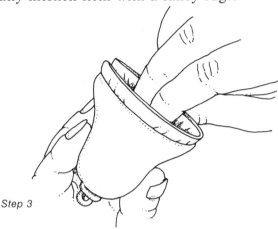

Step 3

Step 4
After your bell is completed to this stage it will need to dry thoroughly for 2-4 days. However, before I leave a bell in a mould for this length of time I tap the sides of the mould and gently let the bell slip out to ensure that it is not stuck to the sides. It is much easier to remove moist paste from a mould than to have to scratch out a bell which is dry but stuck. After you have checked that your bell is free, replace it and allow it to dry. Note that if your bell is very deep you may have to stretch your paste to fit right down to its base.

Step 5
Cornelli work piped on the outside or even the inside of your bell is very pretty and it can hide some of the creases that may occasionally occur in a moulded bell. See cake facing page 54 for an example of these bells. They may be decorated with small flowers or other forms of

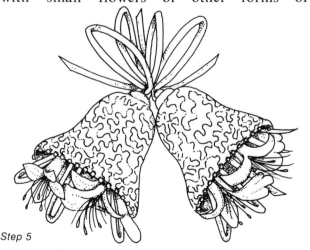

Step 5

embroidery. Flowers spilling out of their centres are lovely and soft as a decoration.

Moulded umbrella

The umbrella on the cake facing page 39 is another beautiful decoration which can be very eye catching. This is also made of gum paste or pastillage. Look for a small curved bowl of a suitable shape and size for your needs.

Step 1
Cut out a template. Then roll out a piece of paste large enough for your bowl. Place the template over this and cut out the umbrella pattern using either a scalpel or an art knife.

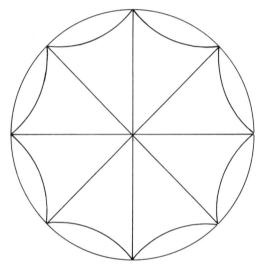

Moulded umbrella — Step 1

Step 2
Dust the inside of the bowl liberally with cornflour, then place the cut-out umbrella into it to take up a curved shape, The outside surface may be used instead if desired. Allow the umbrella to dry for 2-4 days before removing it.

Step 3
File any untidy outer edges which may remain. Then embroider the areas of the umbrella which you plan to decorate. Note that on the umbrella facing page 39 the decorations consist of dots.

Step 4
Make a handle for the umbrella by rolling a piece of paste into a sausage shape. Ensure that

Step 4

it is smooth and long enough for your needs. Shape it to the required curve for the top of the handle and set aside to dry, turning it over occasionally to allow better drying. This also stops the handle from flattening too much.

Step 5
To attach your handle, pipe some royal icing on the end and set it into place on the inside of your umbrella. Support it with cotton wool until dry.

To make a half umbrella (see the cake between pages 30-31) cut only half the circle. Place cotton wool on the underside to support your umbrella in the shape you require. It will not need to set on a bowl. Allow it time to dry before use. The handle to this umbrella is made by piping the outlines, then flooding it in with a watered-down icing (see Floodwork page 39). The handle may be turned over after it is dry and reflooded for extra strength.

Moulded vase

The beautiful spray of flowers facing page 55 consists of a delicate assortment of moulded flowers arranged in a sugar vase. There will be many instances where a vase, a bowl or even a shell may solve a problem in presenting your flowers.

If you prefer a bowl for your arrangement, proceed in the same way as for the umbrella (see page 104).

Step 1
Cut out a circle, either leaving it plain or making a patterned or scalloped edge.

Step 2
Dust the inside of the bowl with cornflour and gently place the piece into the bowl. Ease the paste against the sides and press it gently to take up the shape.

Step 3
This bowl may be altered to a vase by adding a short base after it is dry. The base can be made in exactly the same way, except make the circle smaller so that the second dish shape is shallower. A smaller butter dish may be used to make the base also. Aim for good proportions when selecting sizes.

Step 4
Attach the two bowls together back to back by piping several large dots of royal icing. Then press the two pieces together. Pipe the embroidery or pattern required all over the outside of your vase. A piece of plastic icing

Moulded vase

may be placed inside the vase to attach your flowers securely. Colour your paste before you commence work on items such as these.

Check whether you have any pretty shaped pieces suitable for reproducing in sugar. It is often surprising to see how versatile kitchen items can be. The moulded and decorated plate facing page 38 is made in a similar way to the bowls. The paste should be thicker to give extra strength.

Moulded candle

The candle facing page 55 is made of gum paste and can also be made of pastillage. Take a piece of paste large enough to suit your needs. Roll the paste to a sausage shape. Include in the top a piece of thin cording or a thick stamen cotton. It should remain in place as you roll the paste between your fingers. Trim this 'wick' to a suitable size for your candle. The best way to dry your candle is to allow it to stand upright so that it does not flatten on one side. A long-stemmed specimen vase would be suitable to support the candle gently.

Moulded bible

The bible seen on the cake facing page 95 has been made from gum paste. They can also be made of pastillage. There are two methods which can be used.

Open bible

Open bibles are often requested so that the names of the bride and groom can be piped on the inside of the book.

Step 1
Take a cardboard box, or some plastic or perspex which can be cut to the size and shape required for your book. It is easier to use the base corners of the box to make your shape, using part of one side and part of the base to form an open book shape. Cut the corners to a curved edge if you prefer.

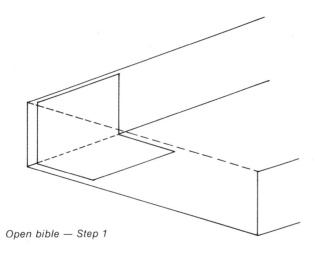

Open bible — Step 1

Step 2
Cut out a piece of waxed paper large enough to cover the cardboard.

Step 3
Take a piece of gum paste, roll it out to a thickness of 2 mm, then cut it to the size of your cardboard and shape the corners.

Step 4
Place the paste on the waxed paper. Then lay it over the open book so that the paste takes up the shape. Pinch the paste a little at the 'spine' of the book to hold the shape a little better. Support this with cotton wool and allow it to dry. To assist with faster drying, the sugar book may be turned over occasionally and placed on the inside of the cardboard to allow the other side to dry evenly.

Step 4

Closed bible

For moulding the closed bible a small book or a piece of cardboard or wood may be used as a pattern.

Step 1
Roll out your paste to a thickness of 2 mm. Cut it to the required size and shape.

Step 2
Then place a suitably sized piece of waxed paper over the book or cardboard. Pick up the paste and gently place it over the cardboard so that it looks like the cover of a book. A skewer or pencil may be used to assist in forming a curved spine.

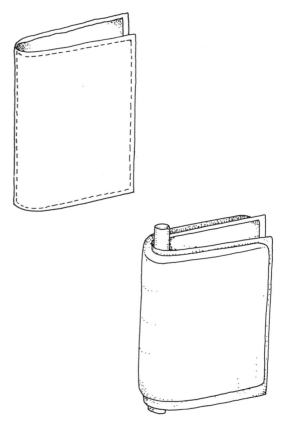

Closed bible — Step 2

Step 3
This paste will take a little longer to dry because one entire side will need to be supported while the other dries. Then reverse the procedure to allow the other side to dry. Cotton wool or foam will be the best thing to rest your book on so that it dries with no pressure marks.

Step 4
A piece of gum paste, rolled to the required size then shaped into a deep curve, can be cut and placed in the book to look like pages. Moisten

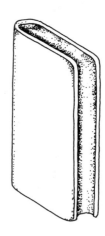

Step 4

the top and bottom edges so that they will set in place firmly. Then place this in the book, starting at the top side. Gently press the paste in place while it is still moist enough to move into the required position, about 5 mm in from the edges of the book.

Step 5
Decorate and colour the book as required for your cake.

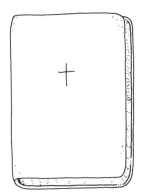

Completed bible

Non-sugar decorations

There are many occasions when decorations other than sugar ornaments can be used with great success. Obviously these items will not be suitable for show cakes, but they will extend your range and offer a pleasing alternative for times when speed and deadlines are important.

Natural objects

Cones, gum-nuts and seed pods, both closed and open, offer a range of possibilities. Jacaranda seed pods, when open and dry, are very attractive. Small cones, casuarina (she-oak) fruits and gum nuts can all be cleaned and allowed to dry thoroughly. Remove the seeds if necessary. These items can be painted over completely with non-toxic gold or silver paint, or the edges may just be tipped lightly. Sugar flowers and leaves may be attached to create very pleasing combinations.

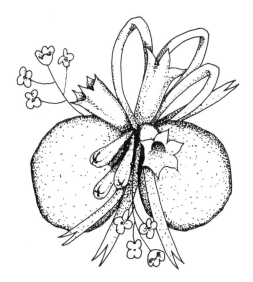

Combined natural and sugar decorations

Cake tins, boards and coverings

Preparation of cake tins

Lining the tins

To ensure a good smooth surface all over, your cake tins should be lined with care. Some decorators do not line cake tins at all when baking a cake. However, having tried both methods, I would recommend that tins be lined, especially for larger cakes.

Depending on the size of the tin being used, and on the thickness of your brown paper, one or two layers of brown and two or three layers of greaseproof paper should be used to line your tins. The larger the tin, the more layers will be needed.

Your paper should be approximately 3 cm higher than the height of the tins. If possible, try to cut all the layers of paper together to ensure that they are uniform in size and therefore easier to handle.

I find that if all the layers of paper are lightly greased with oil or unsalted butter they will stick together and make the task easier. This will reduce problems with layers of paper falling back into the tin and spoiling the surface of the cake. Salted butter is not recommended because the salt increases the chances of the outer edges of the cake burning.

Your lining should be as smooth as possible with no creases or wrinkles. Corners should fit snugly, and not be too tight or too loose.

A circular or oval tin will require two or three pieces of paper for the sides and one for the base.

Hexagonal, diamond and other irregularly shaped tins will require as many pieces as there are sides, and one for the base.

Rectangular and square tins can be lined using one piece of paper, cut in such a way as to line the sides and the base.

When cutting side pieces for lining, allow an extra 3 cm for height over the tin, plus an extra 3 cm to be placed under the base lining. All pieces should overlap by 4-5 cm to allow for the cake mixture to spread during cooking. If the overlap is too long, the mixture will be constricted and therefore badly shaped corners will result. On the other hand, if the overlap is too small the cake mixture will ooze out during baking. The result will be a messy cake with particles baked on either side of the paper.

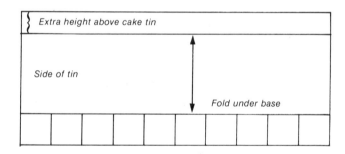

Cutting the lining

To enable side pieces to be tucked in under the base lining, make a 3 cm wide fold on each piece and make a series of cuts 2-3 cm apart along the entire length of each piece. These small cut pieces can overlap to fit snugly around the curve of your tin, or to fit more securely around corners.

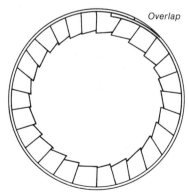

Overlapping the lining

Use the base of your tin for a guide when cutting base pieces. If you place the base lining into your tin and it appears to be too large, remove it and cut off the excess paper.

The lining of tins can be very time-consuming and tedious. However, there will be more frustrations for the decorator if it is not done well.

For lining square or rectangular tins, cut out a piece of paper 6 cm longer and wider than the combined measurement of two sides and the base. Place your tin on the centre and mark out the base measurements.

Now cut four lines into this base area at right angles (see illustration). Grease your lining

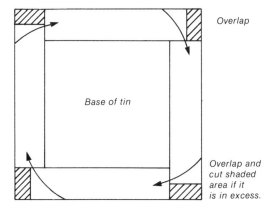

Lining for a square tin

sheets and then lift and snugly fit the base into the tin. You will find that the corners will overlap quite neatly. If the overlap paper is too long, trim it back to the required size.

Note that it is a good idea to make folds in all corner side pieces for all tins so that your lining fits more securely into the corners.

Cake tins will need only the slightest amount of greasing, since the paper is well greased.

Some fancy cake tins will often allow butter to drip and seep from the base. It is a good idea to stand these tins on a flat tray during the long hours of baking time.

Filling the tins

After filling your tin with cake mix, ensure that it is spread up to the corners and packed firmly.

Spread the mixture so that it is even and flat on the top. Use your hands or the back of a spoon. Always drop your filled tin a couple of times on to the bench top from a height to release trapped air bubbles.

Before you place your cake in the oven, smooth the surface of the cake mix. Use a glass of warm water and a metal tablespoon. Dip the

spoon in the water frequently and keep smoothing over the surface of the mixture. This will leave a very fine film of water over the entire top of the cake mix. The result will be a smooth shiny top on your cake, rather than the usual 'moonscape' which is so much more difficult to cover. Leave a slight depression in the centre of the cake, no deeper than the bowl of the spoon. For extra large or long cakes, make two or three of these shallow depressions. These should counteract any minor rising in the centre which often occurs during baking.

Lay a double sheet of foil on top, large enough to overlap the entire cake tin. It will sit on top of the lining, which is higher than the tin, thus allowing for any small amount of cake rising. Leave the foil on the tin for the entire baking time. Your cake will still bake and brown in the usual way.

Baking hints

Cooking times will vary considerably from oven to oven (see directions under recipes on page 128).

After cooking is completed, remove your cake from the oven immediately. *Do not leave your cake in a warm oven until it is cold.*

Before removing the cake from the tin, leave the sheet of foil on top and completely cover the top and sides of the tin with towels or a heavy old blanket for 24 hours. This will result in a beautifully moist, firm cake.

It is best to make the full amount of mixture needed for all the cakes if you are making a tiered cake. It is then possible to divide it evenly so that all cakes will be uniform in height, and no excess height will have to be cut off after baking.

Special tins

Special fancy cake tins are available from cake decorating supply shops and from some large department stores. These tins are usually handmade and are available in sets of graded sizes. Most of the more unusual shapes are very expensive; however, if well looked after, they will last for many years of service.

If unusual tins are required for special occasions, it is sometimes possible to hire these at a reasonable cost from some supply shops, or perhaps you could have them custom made by a tinsmith. Be sure to buy sets of tins with the same shaped corners.

Sizes and proportions

When baking several tiers for a wedding cake, make sure that the proportions are pleasing and look well-balanced. Cakes can often look top-heavy if wrong sizes are matched together. Cakes and decorations should form a good composition which is visually pleasing. No decorator should allow the size of the work to be detrmined solely by the number of people to be catered for. It is always possible to provide another plain covered cake to cater for extra numbers.

Use this triangle as a guide to proportions for your cakes and decorations. All decorations should be scaled to disappear at an imaginary vinishing point at the apex. If the top tier cake is too wide, it will not fit within this triangle. Nor would a spray of flowers which is long and narrow close to the cake, and then wide and heavy at the top.

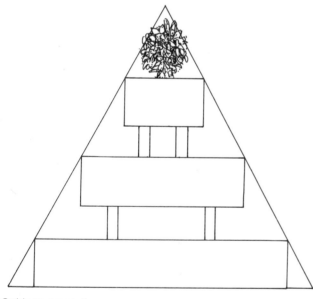

Guide to proportions

For making a tiered cake, a general rule is that there should be a size difference of approximately 5 cm between each layer for a three-tier cake, e.g. 15/20/25 cm or 17/22/30 cm. The difference in width for a two-tier cake should be 7-10 cm, e.g. 15/25 cm or 17/25 cm.

See pages 131-132 for information on amounts of mixture required for different sizes of tins.

If you are unsure as to the size of an unusually shaped cake tin, and therefore do not know what quantity of mixture is required, fill the tin with water up to the usual level and then transfer this to a 20 cm tin to give you a guide. Scale your needs accordingly.

Preparation of boards

Cake boards are often forgotten by decorators. Hours of work may have been devoted to a cake and the most intricate and exquisite decorations may have been used, but if the final product is placed on a board which is either crooked or not well covered all the work will be spoilt.

Plain cut boards are readily available in all shapes and sizes from cake decorating supply stores. These can be purchased already covered with foil in any colour required. The traditional colours are gold or silver but a variety of papers is also available for those who wish to prepare their own boards.

Decorators often make the mistake of not wanting to pay for good boards. This is false economy.

Size of boards

The size of your board will depend on the size of your cake, whether you are making a tiered cake and whether there are to be any decorations actually on the board.

Top tiers should only have between 1.5-3 cm borders around the sides, otherwise they look heavy and also cast shadows over the lower cake.

The base cake can have a wider rim of board. This will add better balance and give more protection. Some decorators also prefer to use a thicker board for the base cake and thinner ones for the top tiers.

Runners

Runners should always be added to the base boards. They enable easier lifting and prevent inadvertent damage to side decorations.

To make runners, lengths of 1-2 cm wide pieces of wood are attached to the underside of the board. Suitably sized wooden curtain rings could be used as a substitute. Use a little wood or hobby glue to attach one at each corner. Do not place these, or the runners, too close to the edge of the board, otherwise they will be visible.

Measuring and cutting

Boards may be cut from suitably thick pieces of masonite, plywood or caneite. To measure the required size for your board, place your cake tins on the sheet of board and trace out the shape from the base of the tin. Now take a compass and ruler and start to measure. Take into account that your cake will be wider than the base of the tin once it is covered with two layers of icing. Decide on the extra width required and mark out dots at the points indicated in the illustration. Note that these markings should be at right angles to the edge of the tin. Shapes can be drawn out with the compass. For angular shapes use the ruler.

Use a good sharp saw to cut the board along the marked lines. Keep these cutting lines straight and even for best results.

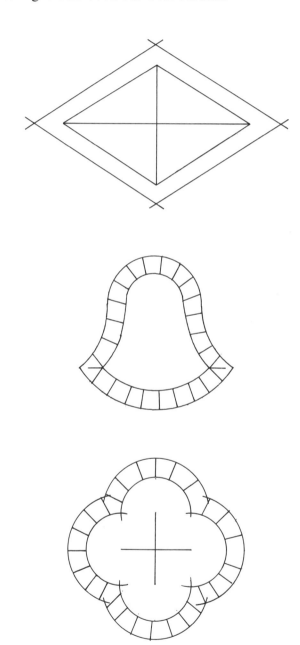

Measuring boards

Covering boards

All boards should have a top and bottom covering. Use silver or gold for the top and white for the base. This will give a more professional appearance. Ensure that your foil is cut large enough to allow for a rim of approximately 4 cm on the underside.

Paper should be pasted all over the board, otherwise it will ripple and decorations or candles placed on the board will break with its movement. Turn your paper upside down. Spread hobby glue or paste all over the paper and a little on the board also.

Place your board over the pasted paper and smooth out the wrinkles. Turn the edges over, then cut sections all around the rim on the underside. Neatly overlap sections where needed and paste them down. Be sure to smooth the paper around the thickness of the sides.

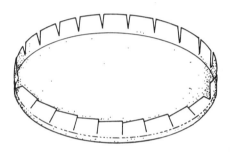

Covering boards

Cut out a suitably sized piece of white paper for the underside. Spread it with glue and paste it down, allowing a small rim of the foil to be visible around the edge. Allow boards to dry thoroughly before use.

When selecting your paper, be sure to choose a colour suitable for your overall colour scheme. Remember to match silver decorations on the cake, such as keys, to a silver board. Do not choose paper which is too bright or has a heavy pattern, otherwise it may make the cake look heavy also. Smooth out wrinkles and remove excess paste by wiping board with a moist cloth.

Covering cakes

Marzipan or almond icing

Not all cakes are covered with marzipan. Almond icing is a more economical choice, and it can be bought commercially or made at home. There are also many reliable imitation almond icings available. No matter which icing you choose, a good foundation covering will enable you to achieve perfect results for your final covering of plastic icing, so time and care are needed.

Step 1
You may use either the top or the bottom of your cake as the upper surface when covering it. If the cake has risen with a peak in the middle, or if it is very uneven, trim off any excess with a sharp knife.

Step 2
Having decided which surface is going to be the top of your cake, start to patch and fill any holes. Marzipan or any scraps of plastic icing may be used for this purpose. Work the icing a little to soften it first. If there are any large gaps, fill these by rolling out some icing to a sausage shape. Place this where required and push into shape with a flat knife. Use a little warmed apricot jam brushed into the holes to ensure the icing remains in place. Sometimes corners on a square cake may need to be packed in this way to give them a better shape.

Step 3
Use a tape measure to measure the top surface of your cake. Check that it is level by using a spirit level on both the top and the sides. Pack with more icing if needed.

Step 4
Brush the heated apricot jam all over the top of the cake. A knife will do just as well for this.

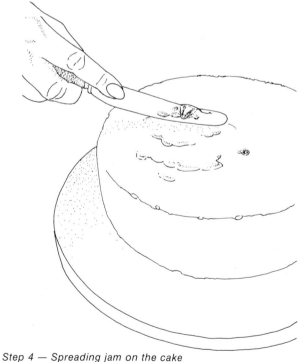

Step 4 — Spreading jam on the cake

Step 5
Measure the quantity of marzipan or almond icing required for the size of your cake (see page 129 for a list of suggested quantities). Knead

your icing a little to soften and make it more pliable. Pull out or cut out any dry hard particles, otherwise you will have lumps in the surface of the cake.

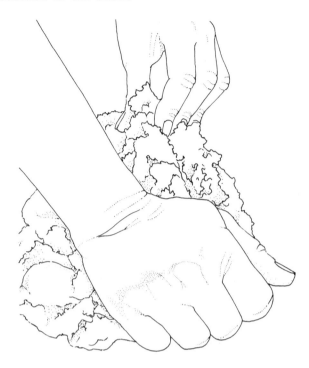

Step 5 — Softening the marzipan

Step 6
Divide your icing into one third and two thirds. Set the larger piece aside.

Step 7
Roll out the smaller piece of icing to a thickness of about 5 mm to the size required. Be sure it is not stuck to the board.

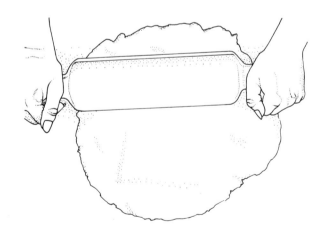

Step 7 — Rolling out the marzipan

Use cornflour on your hands, rolling pin and board to avoid sticking. (Icing sugar is usually recommended for this purpose. However, I find this tends to get sticky, and at times the icing may be gritty. Try both methods to see which one best suits your needs.)

Step 8
Pick up the cake and place the top face down on the rolled-out icing. Make sure that it is placed in the centre and that the icing is large enough for the size of your cake. If you notice any large gaps between the cake and icing, fill them in with extra marzipan.

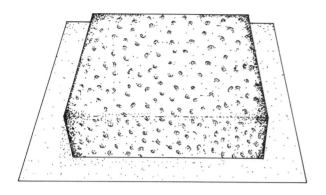

Step 8 — Placing the cake on the icing

Step 9
Cut off excess icing from around the sides of the cake, using either a sharp knife or a firm scraper. Allow an edge of 2 to 5 cm of icing. You can scrape this a little way up the side of the cake for a smooth, even surface. If there are many corners on your cake, use two scrapers — one on each side — to achieve an even finish.

Step 10
Place another board on top of the cake. Pick up the cake, which is now sandwiched between two boards, and turn it over. Gently remove the top board. You will now see a beautifully even top covering.

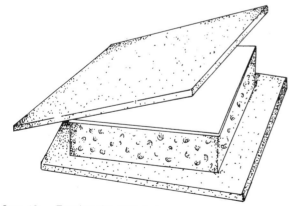

Step 10 — Turning the cake over

Step 11
Measure each side of your cake and cut out a pattern from a piece of greaseproof paper. Allow for the height of the icing to be included. If you have a circular cake, make two or three pieces, depending on its size. A small cake may be done with one piece only.

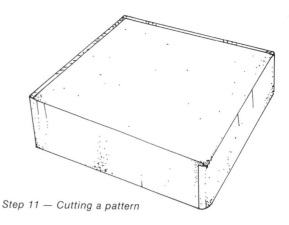

Step 11 — Cutting a pattern

Step 12
Take the icing you have set aside, using enough to cover one side at a time. Roll it out in the same way as before. Place the paper pattern over the top and cut it to the required size.

Step 13
Brush warm jam over one side of the cake, including the side edge of the top icing. Pick up the icing, using the paper pattern for support. This also stops the icing from stretching too much. Place it along one side, making sure that it is even at the bottom of the cake and that it fits snugly up to the top also. Ease it gently with your fingers if it is a little short. Using your scrapers, one in each hand, press against this side with the right hand and the opposite side with your left hand. This will ensure the icing is securely in place, and will also smooth out any wrinkles or finger marks.

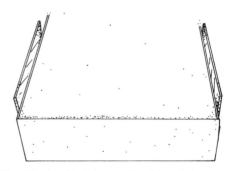

Step 13 — Placing the icing on the sides of the cake

Step 14
Repeat this process for each side piece. For a round cake, brush the edges of each piece with jam to allow them to stick together. For a square cake, the edge of a side piece of icing will stick to part of the inner side of the next piece (see diagram).

When all the sides are covered, press over all the sides once more to remove any marks left in the surface of the icing. If your side pieces of icing are too high for the cake, cut off the excess with a *sharp* knife, drawing it to the centre of the

Step 14 — Edges on a square cake

cake so that edges do not fray and pull away. Do not cut off icing from the top covering.

Plastic or fondant icing

Plastic icing, otherwise known as fondant icing, can be made or purchased. It is the final covering placed on rich fruit cakes. It is also used on other cakes to achieve particular effects. (See recipe for plastic icing on page 129.)

Step 1
Before you start working with the plastic icing, measure the distance over the cake with a length of string or a tape measure. Starting at the base against the board, measure up one side of the cake, across the top and then down to the board on the other side. Knot the string to mark the correct length.

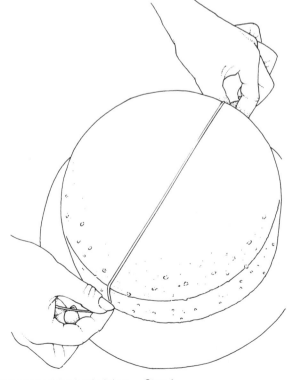

Covering with plastic icing — Step 1

Step 2
Measure and weigh the amount of icing required for your cake (see page 129). Knead the plastic icing thoroughly. Before rolling it out, sprinkle a little cornflour on the pastry board or sheet.

Step 3
Shape your icing into a ball with all join and crease marks on the underside, so that they are not visible when the icing has been rolled out. Roll out the icing with a long rolling pin until approximately 4 mm thick. (Rub a little cornflour on the rolling pin to prevent it sticking.) From time to time, carefully lift your plastic icing and turn it around (not over). It is a good idea always to roll your icing in the shape of the cake you are covering; for example, if you are covering a round cake, start with a ball and roll, lifting and turning constantly, keeping the icing in a circle.

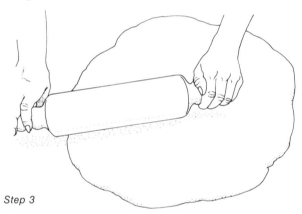

Step 3

Step 4
Give the icing a good 'polish' with your hand by rubbing in a circular motion until it feels and looks like satin. Prick any air bubbles with a thin needle and then rub again to remove the mark. Measure the icing with your piece of string to make sure it is the right size.

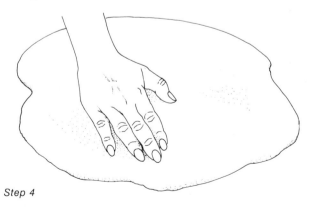

Step 4

Step 5
Brush egg white all over the marzipan covering on your cake.

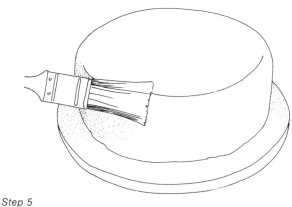

Step 5

Step 6

Cut out the icing you have rolled to the size measured on your string. You may allow an extra 3 cm all around if you wish.

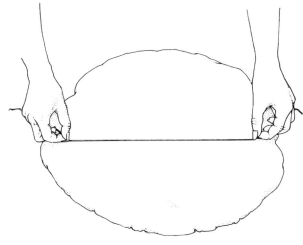

Step 6 (i)

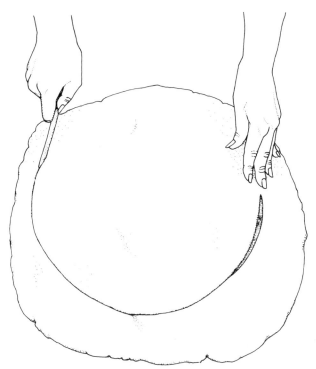

Step 6 (ii)

Step 7

Place your long rolling pin over the top of the icing and roll some of it onto the pin, working from the top to about halfway down. Lift the icing up with the rolling pin. Place the lower edge of the icing against your cake so that the icing is being held over the middle of the cake and just touching the base of the board.

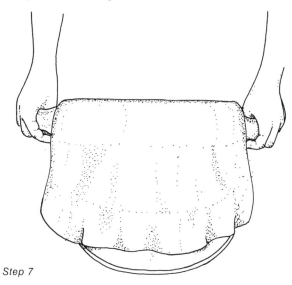

Step 7

Step 8

Unroll the icing, allowing it to fall gently onto the cake as you move the rolling pin gradually across it. Ensure that the icing will cover all of the cake. If it becomes apparent that you have misjudged the placing of your icing, pull it off the cake, re-knead and try again. Any traces of egg white will work back into the icing.

Step 9

Now that the icing is on the cake, work quickly but with care. Gently roll over the top of the cake with your rolling pin to improve the finish. Ease the icing against the sides all around the cake, starting with the corners if the cake is square. Do not press pleats or folds into the icing. Gently press the icing with the palms of the hands. Be firm, but at the same time do not press too hard with your fingers, otherwise you will find the icing has finger marks and thin patches.

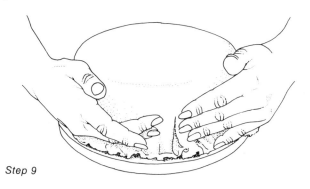

Step 9

Step 10
If your icing appears to be drying very quickly and crazed stretch marks are appearing, especially at corners and at the top edge, use your left hand to lift part of the icing up from the side. At the same time push the icing slightly towards the centre of the cake, while your right hand is used to press the icing against the top edge or corners. It may take a little practice to get the feel of this, but it does improve the surface of the icing. Do this also if the icing is limp because it is too warm.

Step 11
Press the icing around the sides of the cake gradually, working down all sides at the same time. In this way there is a minimum of pull from the weight of excess icing. This is especially important to reduce crease and fold marks.

Step 12
Once the icing has been worked down to the base of the cake and the excess is resting on the board, you may trim this away either with a knife or with your scrapers. Do not cut the icing right to the edge of the cake, because it is sometimes easy to cut off too much. Start by allowing an extra centimetre, then gradually work back to about 2 or 3 mm. Finally press this against the edges of the cake with your scrapers or knife.

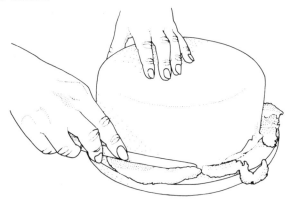

Step 12 (i)

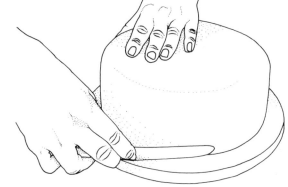

Step 12 (ii)

Step 13
Be careful not to allow too much excess icing to remain at the base, otherwise you will have a bulge at the bottom. Sides should be smooth and even, at right angles to the board.

Step 14
With both hands, rub gently around the sides of the cake and then, using one hand, rub in a circular motion on the top. Do this until the plastic icing feels and looks like satin, but do not press too hard as this may result in thin patches.

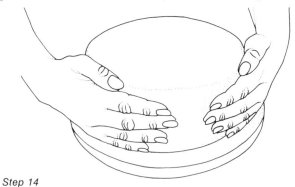

Step 14

Step 15
If you have both heavy and light scrapers available, or perhaps metal and pliable plastic ones, use both sets to achieve a good finish to your cake. Heavy or metal scrapers allow you to press more firmly to remove any marks.

Step 16
Before you finish off the sides of the cake, place a spirit level across the top to ensure that it is still perfectly even. If it is not, use your rolling pin gently to roll out any unevenness in the icing. This will also ensure the icing has no finger marks.

Step 17
Using both sets of scrapers, press around the sides of your cake until all marks have gone. Start with your heavy scrapers first; the soft pliable scrapers may then be bent to run gently over the edges and corners of the cake to give it a soft even finish. Should air bubbles have formed, prick them with a sewing needle, but insert the needle at such an angle that when you rub the icing, the prick mark disappears.

Some final tips on covering

Never store icing in a hot cupboard, otherwise it will be hot, limp and stretchy when you use it.

Do not work in a draughty room. This can cause the icing to craze when it is rolled out.

Do not over-work your icing. This applies when you knead it and also when you are smoothing it over your cake. It makes the icing more difficult to handle.

Icing may be removed from a cake and reapplied if you have made a mistake and are unhappy with the result.

Remove rings from your fingers to eliminate the possibility of marking your icing surface. Long nails will also mark your icing.

If possible, store your icing in a double layer of dark, firm plastic bags. Do not use fine, soft plastic because it will harden your icing.

Always remove cake particles, fluff, foreign matter or hard lumps. It is false economy to use up dry, hard edges, because they can cause holes and spoil the surface.

If you have completed the cake covering and still have pin holes which were made to remove air bubbles, pipe a small dot of royal icing into the hole, using the same colour as the covering. Then smooth over with your fingers.

If you have small gaps left on the side of a cake because the icing was not quite large enough, it is often possible to ease and stretch the icing with your fingers to enable it to fit. Work slowly and gently, but do not leave heavy finger marks that cannot be removed.

If you have to work during hot weather, it is better to cover your cake very early in the morning before the heat of the day.

While you are smoothing sides of your cake, if there are too many creases appearing, lift icing up from the cake with your left hand and then work it back down with the other hand. This will stretch away some crease lines.

Save scraps of icing for patching cakes.

Do not store your icing in the refrigerator.

Be sure that your cake is well cooked, otherwise there could be a yeast reaction and your icing may bubble and burst.

Boiled fruit cakes are not suitable for covering with almond and plastic icing because a yeast reaction can occur.

If your plastic icing feels very dry or difficult to work with, try adding 1 teaspoon of pure glycerine for every 1 kg of icing. Knead the icing well before using it; this will help give your icing more elasticity and reduce craze lines.

The covered cake

After your cake is completed, set it aside in a dust-free place for a week or two to allow it to dry thoroughly. It may be transferred to a suitable cake board either immediately after it is covered or after it is completely dry. (See page 110 for preparation of boards.)

Mark the board carefully to show the exact position of the cake. Spread some royal icing to help hold the base of the cake in place.

To ensure no marks are left on the sides of your cake when you lift it onto the board, use two long, heavy cake lifters and also your scrapers. Gently ease the cake from the board by running a knife under the edges. Place one cake lifter on the left and the other on the right side of the cake. Lift and place it in the correct position on the previously marked board.

Now use a scraper against the side of the cake where you are going to remove the cake lifter. Hold it flat against the side of the cake while pulling the cake lifter out from beneath the cake. This will ensure that no icing is broken or pulled away from the edges. Repeat this on the other side when removing the second cake lifter.

If your cake is to be stored during wet or humid weather, place some silica gel crystals in a small container and leave it nearby. These will absorb any moisture and stop the cake from going shiny.

Do not store your covered cake in a plastic container because cakes will sweat and your icing will bubble and lift off. Cardboard or metal tins are better for long-term storage.

Crimping

Crimping, otherwise known as clipper work, is effective, easy to do and very quick.

Notes to remember

Do not use this work excessively, otherwise cakes can take on a hasty 'commercial' look.

Dip the ends of your crimper into cornflour every time you have pressed into the icing. This will prevent icing sticking to the ends.

Always open the crimper before pulling it up from the icing, otherwise you will inadvertently pinch off pieces of icing.

Crimp only freshly applied icing to avoid cracking.

Place a rubber band or piece of elastic about mid-way down the length of the crimper to hold the ends at an even spacing of about 5 mm. This will result in an even effect with no ugly drag marks.

Crimping can be done on any part of a cake. It is very popular for use on edges and around the sides of a cake. There are many designs available, including single and double scallop, 'V' and straight. Start with a couple of basic designs and then extend your range after you become proficient in their use.

Step 1

Put a strong elastic band around the crimper to keep the ends about 5 mm apart. Insert the crimper into the icing. Press the ends together until there is about 2 mm between them Open the crimper slightly and remove them.

Keep dipping the ends of the crimper into cornflour to prevent them from sticking to the icing.

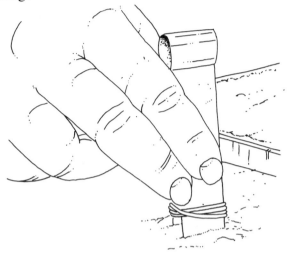

Crimping — Step 1 (i)

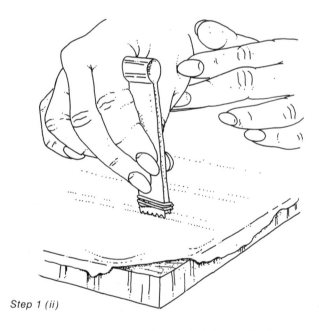

Step 1 (ii)

Use a practice piece of plastic icing rolled out on a board to experiment with different effects. Crimp one row with your 'V' crimper and one row of single scallops. You may now wish to see what effects can be achieved by piping designs on or near your crimper work.

Step 2

Place a No. 00 writing tube into a piping bag and fill with royal icing suitable for writing. Pipe a line or a running dot line on top of the raised part of your crimper work. This may be done using white or coloured icing.

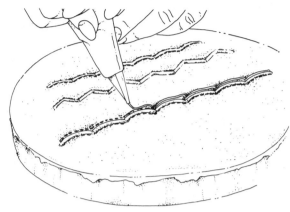

Step 2

Step 3

Three graded dots can be piped at the points where the scallops meet on your row of single scallops.

Step 4

Pipe a line at the point where the 'V's meet, then make two angled lines slightly shorter on either side of the first. Make a dot at the end of each line.

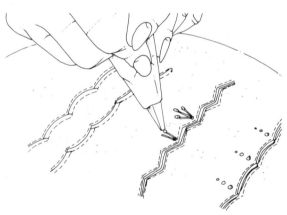

Step 4

Step 5

An alternative pattern, of three dots piped together and then a forget-me-not, could be placed beween the spaces of the pair of scalloped lines.

Facing: This cake consists of three cakes which have been attached together and then covered in sections. The black dragons heads and scrolls are all made of sugar. The tassels are a combination of moulded sugar beads and piped pieces for the lower part. They are attached together with red ribbon. The soft blue velvet base adds a gentle contrast to the softer tones of the flooded side designs. This prize-winning cake was made by Mrs Shirley Vass.

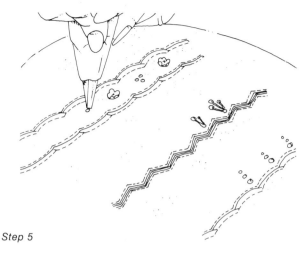

Step 5

Crimping designs

Step 6

The raised part of the icing may be *double crimped,* by crimping over it again in the same way as before. This will give a very fine line or scallop which stands out from the cake. These scallops can be pushed down a little in the centre, or you may wish to press down the points where the scallops meet. A hat pin or a fine skewer will do for both of these effects. In this way you have accentuated the scallops even more. A double row of these is pretty at the base edge of a cake.

Try some of the following designs (see illustrations) for further use on your cakes.

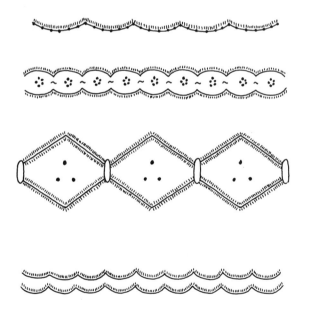

Facing: This delightful bonsai was made by Mrs Maureen Jenkins. It is all made of sugar, including the Japanese lady. The base is a covered fruit cake made to look very realistic with pebbles and moss. The tree has a central support of wire and is packed with fondant. The stems are also made of wire and curved to the correct angle, then flooded with royal icing. The leaves are made of sugar and coloured in natural tones.

Ribbon

Ribbon is often used on cakes. It is a very versatile decoration and is suitable for any occasion.

Fine narrow ribbon is the most popular choice for cakes, although wider ribbons are sometimes used around the side of a cake as a band. It is well worth buying a roll of very fine ribbon in white to keep for future use. This ribbon can be tinted to suit the occasion or to match particular items worn by a bride or bridesmaid.

To tint ribbon, measure the length required. Take a small bowl of methylated spirits and, using an eyedropper, add a few drops of the selected colour. Stir this well, then place the length of ribbon into the bowl of coloured methylated spirits. Allow it to stand for a minute or two, then pull the ribbon out and pat it dry between paper towelling. If the result is not dark enough, repeat the process, adding a little more colour to the methylated spirits.

(This method of colouring is also suitable for any of the flowers made from royal icing, especially if you want very dark colours. Use a very small quantity of methylated spirits for best results with dark colours. Moulded flowers can also be coloured in the same way. However, do not let them stand in the spirits for too long and be sure that they are completely dry before placing them into the fluid. Lay the flowers on towelling to absorb excess moisture. Note that methylated spirits evaporates quickly, so allow for this when colouring several items.)

Loops, bows and longer tails are often used to soften sprays of flowers.

Loops

To make loops, take a length of ribbon. Make three or four loops of the length you require. The ends may be left the same length as the loops, or longer if a tail effect is required. Wrap a piece of wire around the base of these loops and then twist the ends of the wire to form a stem to insert into your cake. Do not leave the wire too long, otherwise it will go through the icing to the cake surface. Cut the ends of the ribbon to a pointed or 'V' shape. Several of these clusters of loops may be needed for larger sprays of flowers.

Bows and knots

These are usually very small when used on a cake. Make them in the usual way. However, instead of trying to make them with a short length of ribbon, it is far easier to use a longer piece and just pull the bow back to a smaller size. To attach them, place a dot of royal icing on the back of the bow and place it where it is required. A pin may be used to hold it in place until the icing has set. *Do not forget to remove all pins.*

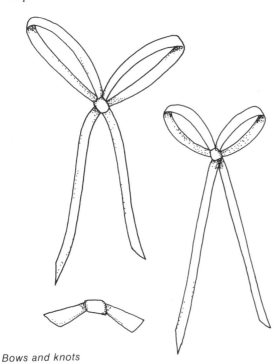

Bows and knots

Insertion

Ribbon may be used in small pieces inserted into the plastic icing on a cake (see facing page 31). This method is very pretty and quite simple to do.

Ribbon insertion

Bands

You may also place ribbon in bands around a cake, or in small lengths across corners on a square cake. Sometimes two or three coloured

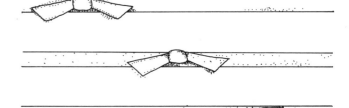

Ribbon bands

ribbons may be used for a particular colour scheme. Two rows of ribbon may be placed with a small space left between. This space may be embroidered or some very small moulded flowers may be attached.

Two bands of ribbon

To attach ribbon to the plastic icing, pipe several dots at regular spacings and then place ribbon where it is required.

Attaching the ribbon

To help hold the ribbon in place until the icing dries, hold it down with pins. *Always count the number of pins you have used and check that they have all been removed after the icing has dried.*

To secure the ends, just overlap and join with icing. Bows and knots are made separately and attached at these joins. It is not very successful to make a bow with the same piece of ribbon you have placed around a cake. Do not place your ribbon on a cake until the icing is quite dry, otherwise the icing will develop a bulge.

Tulle

Tulle is another popular choice for addition to a spray on cakes. However it is easy to over-decorate with tulle, so be careful to limit the quantity used.

Fans

To make small fan-like shapes, cut your tulle to the required rectangular shape. Fold it backwards and forwards to give a pleated concertina effect. Now cut a semi-circular shape at the top of each end. These scallops may face up or down, but make both sides the same shape. Take a piece of wire, wrap it around the centre of the pleats and then twist the ends together. Cut off any excess wire. Pull open the fan and spread your tulle as needed, either fully open in a fan shape or folded up fairly closely.

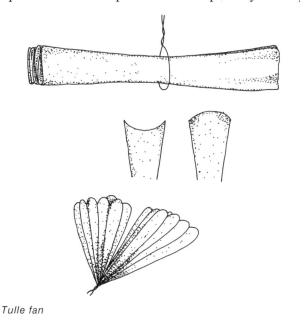

Tulle fan

Handkerchiefs and butterflies are also a popular choice for decorations. The best tulle to use for this purpose is stiffened cotton tulle. Failing this, there is a stiff tulle available for use on cakes from cake decorating supply stores.

Butterfly

Place a piece of tulle the required size and shape over a small rolling pin or other item to achieve the desired effect. A piece of waxed paper is helpful if placed underneath the tulle to avoid breakages. With soft royal icing of writing consistency, pipe along the outer edges of the tulle with a running dot line or whichever pattern you need. Mark out wings with patterns.

Tulle butterfly

Set this aside to dry, then turn over each piece and repipe over the back of the work. Butterfly wings are attached separately to a body. For the body, use a very firm royal icing. Using a No. 0 writing tube, pipe a large dot for the head. Then pipe a line for the body. Repeat this line to thicken it up, but ensure that it is attached to the head. Attach wings before the icing dries. Long feelers may be piped directly on the head once the icing has dried.

Handkerchief

These are only very small and usually have a piped scalloped edge with just a small design at one corner. Be sure to shape your tulle as required before you pipe on it, and be careful not to move the handkerchief too much, otherwise some of the icing will fall off. This is a popular decoration for a cake for grandparents.

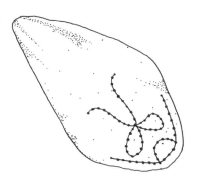

Tulle handkerchief

Assembly, colouring and presentation of cakes

Presentation of moulded flowers

This is the aspect of cake decorating which causes the greatest concern to both the novice and the experienced decorator. Often beautifully made flowers are presented in unflattering arrangements. The work is spoilt because the untidy, heavy bases of flowers, wires at all angles and large blobs of royal icing attaching flowers to the cake are all visible. The 'workings' of any arrangement must always be carefully camouflaged.

To begin with, if the flowers you have made can be wired together in small or medium sprays, it is well worth the effort to do so. This will take a little more time and care, but it can also reduce the number of flowers required, so it may be a saving in the long run.

Assembling a spray

When assembling a spray, it is handy to have a selection of coloured florist's tape, large and small scissors, extra lengths of fuse wire, cotton-covered wire in thick and thin and a sheet of cotton wool or foam to work on.

Take note of how the real flowers look on their stems to give you an idea of what to do. The general rule which applies to any flowers is that the smallest flowers should be placed at the tip of the spray. Two or three sprays can be interwoven to create a fuller effect. Sprays can also be placed back to back or end to end.

Select the colour tape which best suits your colour scheme. For example, if briar roses are to be wired, select a deep green to complement the green of your leaves. This colour will also highlight the soft pale tones of your flowers by giving them a good contrast.

Hold the smallest bud in your left hand. Take a piece of florist's tape which you have already stretched. Hold the end just at the base of the bud where the wire is attached. Wrap just enough tape to hold it securely. Then rest the wire in the centre of the length of tape. Roll the wire between your fingers so that the wire becomes encased in the tape. You fingers will roll the tape around to a smooth even-looking stem. Use a minimum of tape, or the flower stems will be very heavy looking. It is not always necessary to cover the entire length of every wire, because as each bud, leaf and flower is assembled into a main spray, the lower part of the stems are taped to the next piece to create a single stem. Cover or tape the stems of three leaves in the same way as described above.

Using your stretched tape again, wrap the three leaves together so that they look like a stem of leaves on a rose bush, allowing for spaces between each one Tape along only a short length of the stem. Now insert a bud and continue taping a little way further down the stem. Place a wired briar rose at a suitable point

Assembling a spray

along this stem, then continue taping until you have attached all these wires together into one stem. This is now covered with florist's tape. Follow this pattern to assemble all the pieces you wish to use. Naturally some of these stems or sprays may have more buds, flowers or leaves.

Arranging sprays

The arrangement of these sprays of flowers will depend on the size and shape of the cake being decorated. It will also depend on how many flowers you wish to use. The following ideas are only suggestions. Personal taste will be the best choice, but for those who are uncertain, this will be a starting point.

If your cake is a suitable size and shape, try this method of arrangement. Make up two or three arrangements as illustrated. Then place them on the cake so that the lower stems from each spray can be hidden under the previous spray. This is done by placing the first spray on the cake in the desired position. Take the second spray and place it so that the stem is under the larger flower with leaves running in the opposite direction to the first one. If there are any untidy looking spaces, these may be filled by placing single loose flowers where necessary. The stems to these flowers should be hidden. You can cut them very short, then insert the cut end a short way into the icing. Or you can wrap the short stem around the larger stem of the spray.

Stems on the spray may be cut if they are too long. Loops and tails of ribbon may be substituted if preferred. Allow some of these loops to interweave through the spray to soften its appearance.

A pleasing arrangement

Finally, anchor these sprays so that they do not fall off the cake. Take a short length of the cotton-covered wire, loop this to form a few short 'U' shapes, then place them over the stem of each spray and press the lower ends into the icing surface. Be sure not to have these ends too long, otherwise they will make unsightly holes in the icing and also penetrate through to the cake. Ensure that these anchoring pieces of wire can be hidden under the flowers or leaves, or place an extra flower over them so they are not visible. Secure the flowers in several places so that they do not fall off.

Sprays may be made as large or as small as required. They may be dropped over the sides or corners of a cake. Smaller flowers may be added between foliage. If these smaller flowers have stems, they may be taped together in the same way as for the briar rose. Perhaps cut the tape in half lengthwise so that the stems do not become too bulky. Some may be taped together with one piece of tape if they are very fine. Alternatively, small flowers may be held together in very small sprays by assembling them as required, then wrapping and twisting a small length of fuse wire at the base to hold them together.

Allow a short length of wire to remain so that it can be inserted in the icing if required. When these smaller sprays are included between the larger ones, ensure that the bases of the stems are hidden by placing them under leaves or flowers. Pipe a very small amount of icing if needed in any areas. Small sprays of lily of the valley only require a small dot of icing to hold them in place. Place the icing on the underside of the stem, then hold in in place for a minute or two with the end of a pair of tweezers. Brush away any excess icing before it dries.

Do not make large unsightly holes in your icing to attach flowers to a cake. It is not a good idea to make holes into which the base of your flowers are inserted. Flowers should have a soft flowing grace, not a hard stiff effect, and should lie as naturally as possible.

If sweet-peas are to be wired together to form a spray, do so in the same way as for briar roses, but use the three stages of flowers in each spray. No leaves will be required. If your sprays look too empty and need more fullness, lay one spray over the other, then space the flowers so that they interweave with each other. Stems may be bent in any direction needed, just as the flowers and buds can be bent at various angles. Sweet-peas can be arranged and attached in the same way as briar roses.

Arranging flat flowers

For flat flowers, or flowers not wired, your arrangement will have to be done in a different way. The following suggestions are also suitable for making an arrangement which is going to be used as a table centre piece or sold separately.

Take a piece of plastic or fondant icing. The size will depend on the size of your arrangement. If it is to be small, a piece the size of a golf ball will be adequate. Decide whether your arrangement is to be in the shape of a posy. If you prefer a longer look, shape the icing into a boomerang or 'S' shape. Allow this icing to have some height; say 3-6 cm at its highest level. Make some ribbon loops or tulle fans. Insert these on the icing by pushing the wire ends into it. Now take your largest fully open flowers. Pipe some royal icing on the back of each one and start to arrange them on the icing. Remember that these arrangements are to be seen from all angles, so they should be arranged to allow for this.

Do not place one large flower right at the top in the middle, but perhaps take two of your larger flowers and place them almost back to back and tilting down a little so as to soften their effect. Continue arranging so that loops become interspersed with flowers.

Remember to place leaves and buds. Leave some of the smaller flowers to be placed at the two lower edges for a softening effect. Tape the smaller flowers together to form little sprays and insert these wherever they are needed. Use them at the outer extremities also to give an illusion of extra length.

Arrange enough flowers to ensure that the base icing cannot be seen once the arrangement is complete. These arrangements can be placed into suitable sugar cases or bowls or set onto small plaques. Do not forget to shape your arrangements to suit the shape of your cakes.

Assembly of tiered cakes

Tiered cakes are usually assembled by using sugar or plastic pillars. Suitably sized glasses, plastic stands or large wood blocks may also be used. There is no need to restrict the presentation of a cake to the traditional methods, unless of course it is a case of restrictions placed on show entries.

Hints

The following hints may help you avoid some of the usual pitfalls of the inexperienced decorator.

Boards

Remember to attach your cakes to the board they are placed on. This may be done by placing some royal icing under the cake before it is finally covered or before it is transferred to its final board.

The boards used on the top tiers of cakes should not be much wider than the cakes, otherwise heavy dark shadows detract from the decorations on the lower tiers.

The base board may be thicker than the others to support the extra weight.

Pillars

When pillars are used, the tiers do not stand directly on the pillars. They only appear that way. Skewers are placed inside each pillar to bear the weight of the tiers. These should be inserted through the cake, using the pointed end to make the hole. They are then removed and re-inserted with the flat end of the skewer going down to the base of the cake. Place a pillar over this. Mark a line on the skewer 2-3 mm above the top of the pillar. Mark and number each skewer in this way. Then remove them once more and cut the excess off. Be sure that the top surface of each skewer is perfectly flat and level.

Flat flower arrangement

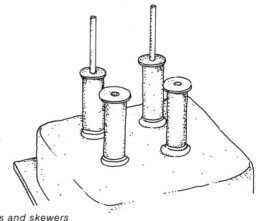

Pillars and skewers

Your cake board for the next tier stands on these skewers. If the cake were placed straight onto the pillars, the weight would either shatter the pillars or make them sink into the lower cake.

'American style' cakes do not sit flat on top of each other as they appear to do. Each tier has skewers through the lower cakes. These are cut 2-3 mm higher than the cake and then the next layer sits on these.

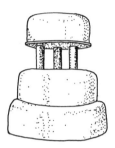

American style cake

Heart shaped cakes require 3 pillars for each layer. Oval cakes require 3 or 5. Round cakes should also have 3 or 5 pillars.

Heart shaped cake

Round cake

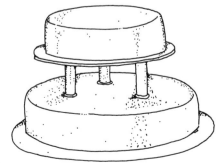

Oval cake

Ensure that the seams of your pillars are all facing to the inside of the cake.

If your cakes are to be placed on one large board, ensure that all stands being used are firm and stable.

The simplest method to establish where pillars should be placed is to cut out a template of each cake. This can be done by tracing out the base of each cake either from the cake or the tin. If the tin is used, allow for the extra thickness of the icing. Using your ruler, mark out on each piece of paper where each cake should have its pillars placed. If you are making a three-tier cake, the pillars should be placed under each other but each layer will have them spaced further apart.

Spacing in the long run will have to be determined by balance, but if pillars are placed about 3-4 cm from the outer edge of the top of each cake this should offer plenty of support.

Be sure that your pillars are even and straight. They may be sanded down with fine sandpaper to remove any uneven edges. If you are making your own pillars, be sure that they are all the same and of the same height, otherwise your cake will be uneven.

Composition

Do not forget good balance and composition when deciding how to arrange your cakes, especially if the cakes are going to be assembled individually at different heights on one large board. It may be necessary to arrange a spray of flowers or some sugar ornaments to the large board to give a final touch.

Transporting

Do not carry your cakes assembled, but lift each tier off and carry separately.

Colouring and shading

Subtle, realistic colouring is of great importance to the final result of a cake. Cakes are made to be eaten, and should therefore not be heavy and sickly in colouring.

Practise colour combinations by pasting a sample of each of the colours you intend using on a piece of paper which is the same colour as your cake. Any combinations which are not suitable can then be altered.

Test your liquid food colours in a glass of water. Add a drop at a time of the various colours you would like to use. Make notes of the results so that you have a reference when you need to mix a particular colour.

Colour wheel

A *colour wheel* (between pages 62-63) will be of great assistance with colour mixing. It is necessary to have instructions and information on its use, otherwise it cannot be used to full advantage.

Remember that red, blue and yellow are primary colours. You must have these three colours to mix any of the others you may need. If you want to keep your colour range to a minimum, these must be included.

Take note that each colour is adjacent to its complementary colour on a colour wheel. If you mix red and yellow together in varying amounts, the result will be all the shades of orange shown *between* those two colours. Yellow mixed with blue will give the range of greens shown between those colours. Red and blue will make purple, in various shades. Green mixed with red will make brown. A drop of all the primary colours will make black. Try these ideas and make notes of your results.

Food colours

Some food colours are very harsh and need to be softened before use. Add a drop or two of caramel to soften them.

If you make a mistake in mixing colours, do not be afraid to start again. If you have made a shade far darker than required, use part of the colour made and add more icing to lighten it.

Each type of colouring available has advantages and disadvantages. Gradually learn to use the one most successful for your particular needs.

Pastels or chalks are very handy for very soft pale shades and for hazy effects, but unfortunately they can sometimes look very patchy.

Liquid food colours are easily mixed. They are very successful for floodwork, but the inexperienced person never fully appreciates how strong they are without first making a mistake.

Paste colours are very good for mixing into icing, and are ideal for use when dark shades are required. However, they are not as good for light pastel colouring.

Powder colours are very messy. The grains float around the room without your being aware of it, until you see little unwanted specks of colour on cakes or equipment. However, sometimes a particular shade is only available in a powder colour, so they may be useful. They are also very economical.

Colouring hints

It is a good idea to use rejects for your colour testing and colour experiments. Do not forget to make notes of what you use so that the result can be repeated when required.

Do not colour any of your work under artificial lighting, because colours will often appear darker in natural light.

If flowers are to be coloured, be very sparing with both the colour and the methylated spirits. Dilute the colour you wish to use. This can be done either with a drop or two of water or with methylated spirits. Then add enough methylated spirits to colour all the flowers. Paint this on with a fine brush. It may be easier to use the larger brush if your flowers are large. Keep a dry cloth close by so that excess moisture may be wiped off the brush before applying it to the flower. This will stop colours from running and spreading further than you need them. Highlights or strong lines required should be painted on with undiluted colour.

It is not possible to blend colours on the flowers. It is better to add colours only where

Facing, above: Made by Mrs Joyce Boyle, this cake has a rich colour scheme of red, green and gold. It is a pretty yet simple design which would be suitable for other occasions beside Christmas. It was exhibited at the Whittlesea Show.

Facing, below: This cake would also be suitable for occasions other than Christmas. Made by Mrs Sylvia Henry, it has been decorated with a pretty arrangement of flannel flowers, wattle, waratah and gum nuts.

Centre left, above: A traditional cake for Christmas, made by Mrs Maureen Ball and exhibited at the Whittlesea Show. Lace, extension work and floodwork are combined to give a pretty and soft Christmas effect.

Centre left, below: This cake, made by Mrs Maureen Kirsch and exhibited at the Whittlesea Show, is a good example of how to decorate a round cake.

Centre right: These chocolate eggs have been decorated with a variety of piped flowers made from royal icing. They also include embroidery and ribbon. All items have been attached with royal icing. The two smaller sugar eggs have been decorated in coloured jelly. This style is suitable for young children. The outlines have been done in chocolate.

and when you are sure of what is needed, as if you were doing a watercolour painting. It is, however, possible to darken tones successfully.

If you have been colouring a piece of floodwork and have spilled too much colour, it is sometimes possible to reflood with icing and and try again. This method may sometimes be necessary for colouring faces.

Very dark colours such as reds need to be strong. It is often easier to work some powder colouring into your paste before you make the flowers, then recolour if needed.

Briar roses may be coloured with very lightly pastel coloured methylated spirits. Colour the spirits to the desired shade of pink, then paint the back of the flower. Be careful not to use a saturated brush, otherwise the colour will creep around the edges and leave marks on the front of the petals.

Sweet-peas may be painted in the same way, except that both sides of the flower will need to be coloured. These flowers may also have the outer edges tipped with with a darker shade to give a realistic effect. Do not saturate your brush with colour, otherwise it will spread over all the flower. Run the colour along the edge of the thickness of the petals.

Flowers such as *daisies, blossom, jasmine* and *frangipani* are best coloured with the dry powder scraped from the pastels or chalks. Brush this powder over the areas which need to be coloured, using a dry brush. This will give the petals a soft dusted look which is very delicate. If there is any excess powder left on the petals, gently blow this off.

A refillable spray bottle or similar item is handy for colouring also. Fill it up with the pastel-coloured methylated spirits, spray each flower and then place it onto a paper towel to dry. Respray any flowers which are not dark enough.

Finally, flowers such as *pansies* which need a combination of effects should be studied closely to establish what the real flower looks like. Each colour will need to be applied from dark to light. Then using a different colour, commence with a pale colour close to the first one. Darken this tone as you work in from the edges and then allow it to fade to a very pale centre. This method is good for gaining experience at colour control.

Often, where dark colours are needed, it is best to use the colour at full strength and then repeat the colouring if it dries steaky or is not dark enough.

Do not colour any sugar items that have a lot of cornflour on the surface, otherwise colours will become patchy.

Do not colour with water only, because this will take longer to dry. It will sometimes remain sticky, and perhaps even dissolve the icing into a hole if too much water is used.

When methylated spirits is used for colouring, the spirit evaporates very fast and allows for repeated colourings if needed. These items are still edible, but they may sometimes have a bitter taste.

Finally, ribbons, stamens or flowers may also be coloured by immersing them into a suitably coloured solution of methylated spirits. Allow the item to dry before deciding if the process should be repeated to darken them further.

Facing: Cone people and other novelties.

Recipes

Icing and paste recipes

(See conversion tables on page 134 to convert metric measure in recipes to imperial measures if you prefer to use these.)

Butter icing

125 g butter
500 g icing sugar
5 ml vanilla essence
125 ml milk, water or fruit juice

Cream the butter very well. Gradually add the icing sugar. Add vanilla essence, but not onto dry icing sugar, then add the liquid sparingly, beating well until the icing is smooth and of a spreading consistency. You may not need to use all the liquid.

Royal icing

1 egg white
250 g icing sugar, sifted four times
acetic acid or lemon juice

Beat the egg white lightly with a fork or wooden spoon until loose and slightly frothy. Add icing sugar, 25 g at a time, beating each addition *thoroughly*. The consistency of the icing should be that of well beaten cream and able to hold small peaks. Add the acetic acid or lemon juice and continue beating. Thicken with icing sugar until you have the necessary consistency. You may not need to use all 250 g of icing sugar.

If mixing by hand, it takes about 15 minutes to mix royal icing. With an electric mixer on medium speed it takes about three minutes.

Royal icing for figure piping

To a batch of royal icing (1 egg white) add 12.5 g meringue powder. The icing should be of a small peak consistency — when piped into a ball or body shape, the icing must hold its shape. If the icing is too stiff, it will form ridges when piped.

Royal icing for extension or bridgework

250 g pure icing sugar, sifted four times
1 egg white
acetic acid or lemon juice as required

Since the icing you require for this work should be free of any hard particles, sift your icing sugar through a piece of silk four times. This is slow, tedious work but well worth the extra time spent. It enables you to work freely without having to keep stopping because of blocked tubes.

Whip your egg white to soft peak consistency, then add icing sugar, one tablespoon at a time, mixing between each addition for three minutes. Finally add the lemon juice or acetic acid if required. If your egg white appears to be insufficient for the quantity of icing sugar, use only the amount required to make an icing which is smooth and free flowing but not too soft.

Boiled icing

125 g butter
60 ml milk
10 ml flavouring (vanilla, peppermint, or any other)
500 g sifted icing sugar
colouring

Melt the butter in a pot and blend in the milk, vanilla essence and 100 g of icing sugar thoroughly with a wooden spoon. Add colouring. Bring the mixture to the boil and remove immediately from the heat. Beat in some more of the icing sugar. Experience will teach you to judge accurately the amount of icing sugar to be added. The consistency of boiled icing should be that of a thick liquid; it should pour easily over the cake and spread on its own.

Pour all the icing over the cake through a metal strainer. If necessary, smooth the icing on the side of the cake with a knife but do not touch the top. Tidy up the plate after a few minutes by removing any excess icing with a knife and then wiping the plate clean with a damp cloth.

Chocolate icing

To make boiled chocolate icing, add 25 g of sifted cocoa when you add the milk, vanilla essence and icing sugar.

Moulding sugar

500 g castor sugar
20 ml cold water

In a bowl, add the water to the sugar and mix using a fork. Make sure that there are no lumps — the sugar should be like damp sand when pressed.

To colour the sugar, colour the water before adding it to the sugar.

Marzipan

Most cake recipe books include a recipe for marzipan or almond paste. The one given here can be made up with the ready-prepared packets of almond paste available at most supermarkets.

2 packets (500 g) marzipan or almond paste
2 egg yolks
25 ml brandy
150 g icing sugar

Thoroughly knead all ingredients together. Roll out and place on the cake already coated with apricot jam. Allow this marzipan to stand for about four days before putting on the plastic icing. Also remember to boil the jam before using it.

Plastic icing or fondant icing

I have tried a number of different plastic icing recipes and have found these two the best and easiest.

Plastic icing 1

1 kg icing sugar (sifted)
2 egg whites
100 ml clear liquid glucose
10 ml cooking oil

12.5 ml lemon juice
1 ml tartaric acid
5 ml gelatine
15 ml water

Combine the water and gelatine and stand in a small bowl of boiling water. Stand the bottle of liquid glucose in hot water. Put half of the icing sugar into a bowl and add all the other ingredients. Work to a smooth paste. Gradually add the other half of the icing sugar and knead until the icing is smooth and easy to roll out.

Plastic icing 2

500 g icing sugar
50 ml liquid glucose
1 egg white

Sift the icing sugar into a basin. Make a well in the centre and add the glucose (softened after standing in a cup of hot water) and egg white. Beat, drawing the icing sugar into the centre, until you have a stiff paste. Turn onto a board lightly dusted with sifted icing sugar, and knead very well.

Icing Quantities

Size of cake	Almond icing	Plastic icing
12-15 cm	500-750 g	500-750 g
17-20 cm	1 kg	1 kg
25 cm	1.5 kg	1.5 kg
30 cm	2 kg	2 kg

Gum paste

Gum paste 1

1 lean tablespoon gelatine
1 level teaspoon cream of tartar
½ cup water
500 g pure icing sugar
1 cup fine sifted cornflour

Stir dissolved gelatine and cream of tartar and water over very low heat. Do not allow the water to overheat, otherwise the gelatine will lose its properties. The liquid will be clear with a small amount of white residue from the cream of tartar. Allow this to cool, then add icing sugar and cornflour. Stir the mixture vigorously, until it feels very sticky. Place a damp cloth over the top for an hour, then stir again. This mixture may now be divided into two or three small plastic containers and placed in the freezer until needed. Use one container at a time. After use, the remainder of gum paste left in the container can be refrozen as long as it has not hardened. Always cover the paste with a fine film of plastic while in use, to reduce drying out. Note that a little more water may be added if your mixture appears to be too dry when it is first made. Allow mixture to mature for 24 hours before using it.

To use this mixture, take a small ball or teaspoon of the mixture. Knead cornflour into the paste until it becomes firm and smooth. It will take up quite a lot of cornflour each time and naturally will increase in volume.

The degree of firmness will depend on what you wish to use it for. Usually flowers requiring hand moulding will need paste a little softer than that for rolling out. It will take a little time to learn what consistency is needed each time. People with very warm hands should make their paste firmer than others, because the heat of their hands will soften the paste. It should feel like plasticine when it is ready to be used. If it looks almost grey in colour, or is tacky and sticky, add more cornflour. Too much paste will result in thick heavy flowers that fall off their wire and break apart. If your flowers have a crazed appearance it is because the paste is the wrong consistency.

The paste will dry quickly on the outside surfaces but still be moist on the inside.

Do not use too much cornflour on your fingers or tile while making your flower. Hands, rolling pin, cutters and tile should only be lightly dusted. It is better to knead the extra cornflour into the paste first. A good idea for easy handling is to use a piece of panty-hose or fine silk (or any other suitable fine fabric) to make a little cornflour bag. Place a few teaspoons of cornflour in the cloth, wrap a rubber band around the top and then just shake over areas where cornflour is required.

Gum paste 2

    750 g pure icing sugar
    1 rounded teaspoon gelatine
    1 rounded teaspoon Copha
    3 dessertspoons water

Sieve the icing sugar into a basin. Dissolve gelatine in water with the Copha over a gentle heat. Add to icing sugar and mix with your wooden spoon. Keep airtight and freeze in small containers. Add more cornflour as it is needed in the same way as for the previous recipe.

Flower moulding or modelling paste

    500 g sifted icing sugar
    25 g gum tragacanth
    12.5 g gelatine
    30 ml cold water
    30 ml boiling water
    1 large egg white
    white margarine or vegetable fat
    new plastic bag

Grease a glass mixing bowl and set it over hot water. Heat icing sugar in the bowl. Add the gum tragacanth and stir with a wooden spoon to heat evenly. Do not let the sugar get moist. Heat to just warmer than bloodheat, then remove from the water.

Prepare the gelatine by sprinkling it onto the cold water. Then add the 30 ml boiling water. Stand the gelatine in a bowl of hot water to dissolve. *Do not* put it near the stove as gelatine must never get too hot.

Beat the egg white lightly with a fork to break it up.

Remove 250 g of warm icing sugar and keep it to one side. Add the dissolved gelatine and most of the egg white to the icing sugar left in the bowl. Stir, mixing quickly and *well*. Now add the remaining icing sugar and beat well. Transfer this to a clean, greased bowl and with clean hands greased with white margarine or vegetable fat, work the paste for 10 to 15 minutes. Add the remaining egg white if the paste seems a little dry or stiff.

If you leave the paste, cover the bowl with a plastic bag or damp cloth.

Shape the paste into a ball, grease the outside with white margarine or vegetable fat and store it in the new plastic bag in a sealed container in the refrigerator.

Once or twice a week take out the paste and work it for about five minutes.

Flower moulding or modelling paste made with plastic icing

    500 g plastic icing
    25 g gum tragacanth
    small quantity of egg white

Mix together and work plastic icing and gum tragacanth thoroughly. Lastly, work in egg white. Store in a plastic bag in an airtight container. This paste improves with age and should not be kept in the refrigerator.

Modelling paste

250 g pure icing sugar
1 lean tablespoon gelatine
30 ml water
1 level teaspoon glucose

Dissolve gelatine in water over gentle heat. Do not overheat, otherwise your gelatine will not work. Add the glucose and stir until mixture is clear. Allow to cool a little, then add this to the sifted icing sugar and stir briskly. Allow to stand with a damp cloth over the top for about an hour. Divide into 2 or 3 plastic containers and freeze. Use as required, adding more icing sugar or cornflour to firm it to the required consistency. This is best used after a few hours.

Piping Jelly

(Alternative to purchased jelly)
This recipe is a substitute for the jelly described on page 42. This is suitable if you have difficulty in purchasing it, although it does not have a very long lifespan.

¼ cup lemon juice
1 level tablespoon cornflour
¼ cup water
4 tablespoons castor sugar

Place all ingredients in a small pan and dissolve over low heat. Stir continually until mixture comes to the boil. Allow it to thicken , then remove from heat. If the mixture thickens too much, add a little more water. Colour as required with liquid food colours. Store in refrigerator.

Cake recipes

Basic fruit cake

250 g (¹/₂ lb) butter mix for 20 cm tin

1 tablespoon marmalade jam
250 g butter
250 g sugar
5 eggs, beaten
250 g plain flour
60 g self raising-flour
pinch salt
1 teaspoon nutmeg
1 teaspoon mixed spice
250 g raisins
500 g sultanas
250 g currants
125 g chopped blanched almonds
125 g mixed peel
125 g chopped glace cherries
1 tablespoon glycerine
½ cup rum, sherry or brandy
(Rum is the best preserver, but sherry may be used for economy.)

Chop nuts and raisins in quarters. Place all fruit and nuts in a large bowl. Pour rum and glycerine over these and allow to stand overnight, or a day or two if you have the time. Stir occasionally to allow all the fruit to absorb the rum. (The glycerine may be omitted if preferred. Its function is to help the fruit to swell to a good full size.)

Sift flours and spices together.

Use your clean hands to mix the cake rather than a mixer. The natural warmth from the hands will help the butter to cream better. Cream butter and sugar, then add marmalade jam. Gradually add the beaten eggs a little at a time.

If your mixture is inclined to curdle at this stage, add a little flour between each addition. (This will prevent the fruit from dropping to the bottom of the cake when it is baked.) Then add half the sifted flours and spices, then half the fruit, then the remainder of flour and fruit. Place into a 20 cm lined cake tin. (See page 00)

Preheat gas oven to 250°C for 20 minutes then bake cake at 140°C for 4 hours.

Preheat electric oven at 160°C for 20 minutes then bake cake at 140°C for 4 hours.

Cooking time may vary from 4 to 5 hours depending on your oven and also on humid weather. If your oven tends to be very hot, perhaps lower it to 120°, especially if you are baking a larger cake.

Scale your mixture according to your needs and to the size of your tins (see chart). I am including a 125 g (¼ lb) and 500 g (1 lb) mixture for your cakes. Mix these in the same way as described above.

125 g (¼ lb) butter mix for 15 cm tin

½ tablespoon marmalade
125 g butter
125 g sugar
3 eggs
125 g plain flour
30 g self raising-flour
small pinch salt
½ teaspoon nutmeg
½ teaspoon mixed spice
125 g raisins
250 g sultanas
125 g currants
60 g chopped blanched almonds
60 g mixed peel
60 g chopped glace cherries
½ tablespoon glycerine
¼ cup rum, sherry or brandy

500 g (1 lb) butter mix for 25 cm tin

2 tablespoons marmalade jam
500 g butter
500 g sugar
10 eggs
500 g plain flour
125 g self raising-flour
good pinch salt
2 teaspoons nutmeg
2 teaspoons mixed spice
500 g raisins
1 kg sultanas
500 g currants
250 g chopped blanched almonds
250 g mixed peel
250 g chopped glace cherries
2 tablespoons glycerine
1 cup, rum, sherry or brandy

Calculating measurements and quantities

The following guide will show you how much basic fruit cake mixture to make for various sizes of tin. These may be square, round or fancy shaped tins.

Size of tin	Cake mixture
15 cm (6 inch) tin 17 cm (7 inch) tin	125 g (¼ lb) butter mix
20 cm (8 inch) tin 22 cm (9 inch) tin	250 g (½ lb) butter mix
25 cm (10 inch) tin	500 g (1 lb) butter mix
30 cm (12 inch) tin	625-750 g (1¼-1½ lb) butter mix (depending on height required)

To assist with measurements and quantities, use a 20 cm round or square tin as a guide. Fill the tin with water to the level required, then measure how many times this will fill the tin you wish to use.

Combine quantities of cake mix according to the size of tins being used for tiered cakes. Note that quantities for 15 and 17 cm tins and for 20 and 22 cm tins are the same. However the larger cakes will not be quite as high as smaller ones.

If for any reason it is necessary to keep costs on a cake to a minimum (for instance if a cake is being donated free of charge), check to see if a smaller cake mix could be baked in the size of tin you require, using the above water method. Sometimes a thicker covering of plastic icing could also reduce costs. However, do not omit almond icing if the cake is to be kept for a long time, as colours from the fruits will seep through the icing.

Cakes for butter icing

The following four recipes may be useful for the decorated cakes under Butter icing (pages 12-13).

Chocolate cake

1 cup castor sugar
½ cup milk
¼ cup hot water
1½ cups self raising-flour
4 heaped tablespoons cocoa
85 g butter
1 egg

Cream butter and sugar, dissolve cocoa in hot water. Add egg and beat. Add half the milk and water, and mix again. Add the rest of the milk, water and flour and beat a little longer until mixture is smooth. Bake in a greased 20 cm cake tin for 25-35 minutes at 180° C.

Egg yolk sponge

This is a good recipe to use up left-over egg yolks after making your royal icing.

  5 egg yolks
  3 tablespoons hot water
  ½ cup sugar
  ¾ cup self raising-flour
  2 tablespoons cornflour
  3 tablespoons hot water, extra

Beat the egg yolks until they are light and fluffy. Add 3 tablespoons of hot water and beat. Slowly add the sugar, flour and cornflour, beating between each addition. Add 3 more tablespoons of hot water. Bake in a pair of greased sandwich sponge tins (17 cm or 20 cm) at 180° for 20-25 minutes.

Chocolate sponge

  4 eggs
  1 cup castor sugar
  1 teaspoon cream of tartar
  ½ teaspoon bicarbonate of soda
  1 cup custard powder
  vanilla essence to taste
  2-3 tablespoons cocoa

Whip egg whites until they are stiff. Add egg yolks and whip again. Gradually add dry ingredients, beating until they are all mixed together. Add vanilla essence. Bake in a pair of greased tins (17 cm or 20 cm) at 180° C for 20-25 minutes.

Plain butter cake

  120 g butter
  ½ cup castor sugar
  vanilla essence to taste
  3 eggs
  ¾ cup of milk
  180 g self raising-flour

Cream butter and sugar. Add egg yolks one at a time. Add flour gradually, then beat in milk and vanilla essence. Whip egg whites separately and fold them into the mixture thoroughly. Bake in a greased cake tin (20 cm or 22 cm) at 180° C for 30-40 minutes.

Fairy cakes

  340 g self-raising flour
  ½ level teaspoon salt
  170 g butter
  170 g sugar
  3 eggs
  ¾ cup milk
  1 teaspoon vanilla essence

This recipe makes approximately 36 fairy cakes, but quantities may be halved if desired.

Sift flour and salt together and set aside. Beat butter, sugar and vanilla together to a creamy consistency. Gradually beat in the whisked eggs. Lightly but thoroughly stir in flour and milk, adding half the flour, then half the milk, then the rest of the flour and the rest of the milk. Lightly grease shallow patty cake tins and fill with a lean tablespoon of the mixture. Bake at 140° C for 15 to 20 minutes. They may also be baked in paper or foil patty cups.

Conversion tables

Weights

Metric	Imperial
15 g	½ oz
30 g	1 oz
60 g	2 oz
90 g	3 oz
125 g	4 oz
185 g	6 oz
250 g	8 oz
500 g	16 oz (1 lb)
1000 g (1 kg)	32 oz (2 lb)

Cake Tin Sizes

Metric	Imperial
15 cm	6 inches
17 cm	7 inches
20 cm	8 inches
22 cm	9 inches
25 cm	10 inches
30 cm	12 inches

Liquid Measures

Metric	Imperial	Household measure
5 mL	—	1 teaspoon
15 mL	½ fl oz	—
30 mL	1 fl oz	1 teaspoon
60 mL	3 fl oz	—
150 mL	5 fl oz	—
250 mL	8 fl oz	1 cup
600 mL	20 fl oz	1 pint

Oven Temperature Guide

	Electric		Gas	
	°C	°F	°C	°F
Low or cool	95	200	95	200
Very slow	120	250	120	250
Slow or warm	150	300	150-160	300-325
Moderately slow	160	325	160-175	325-350
Moderate	175	350	175-190	350-375
Moderately hot	190	375	190-205	375-400
Hot	205	400	205-230	400-450
Very hot	230	450	230-260	450-500

Patterns

Happy Anniversary

HAPPY BIRTHDAY

Seasons Greetings   Best Wishes

Noel   Happy Birthday

GOOD LUCK

Happy Birthday

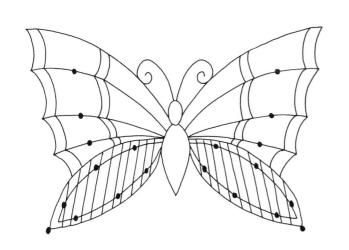

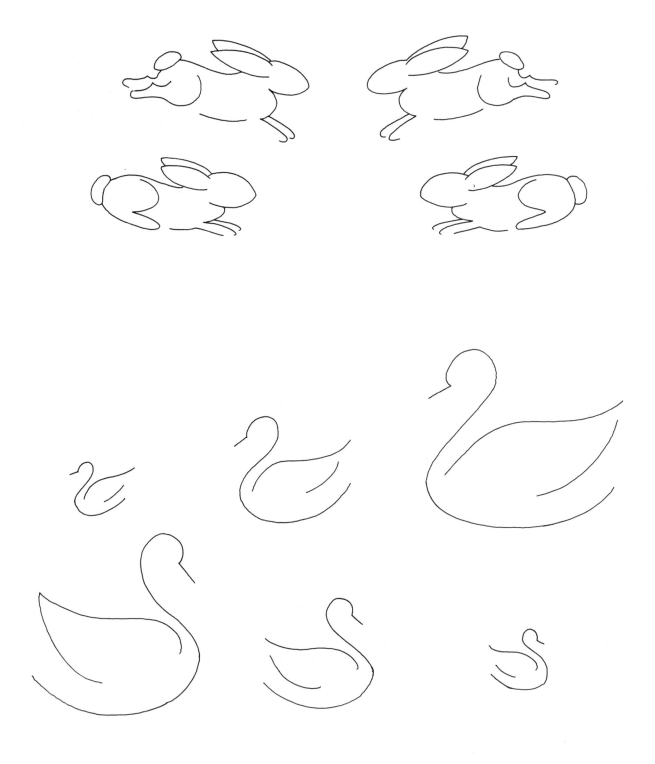

Index

The following cake decorators supplied examples of their work to be photographed for this book:

Mrs Maureen Ball of Victoria
Mrs Noelle Barnard of Victoria
Mrs Cathleen Bowen of New South Wales
Mrs Joyce Boyle of Victoria
Mrs Alice Burnham of Victoria
Mrs Sue Colclough of Victoria
Mrs Nola Cordell of Victoria
Mrs Joy Cornish of Victoria
Mrs Wendy Fox of Victoria
Mrs Maureen Gates of New South Wales
Mrs Sylvia Henry of Victoria
Mrs June Hooper of Victoria
Mrs Rena Hurtado of New South Wales
Mrs Maureen Jenkins of Victoria
Mrs Eva Kidd of Victoria
Mrs Maureen Kirsch of Victoria
Mrs Pam Leman of New South Wales
Mrs Mary Lynas of New South Wales
Mrs Marilyn Lock of New South Wales
Mrs Margaret McGann of Victoria
Mrs Mary Medway of New South Wales
Mrs Robyn Nolan of Victoria
Mrs Heather Oswin of Victoria
Mrs Dorothy Parsons of Victoria
Mrs Constance Russell of Victoria
Mrs Valda Seidel-Davies of Victoria
Mrs Dorothy Silva of Victoria
Mrs Shirley Vass of Victoria
Mrs Pat Welch of Victoria
Mrs Rose Whitehead of Victoria